Published by Jossey-Bass
A Wiley Imprint
989 Market Street, San Francisco, CA 94103-1741—www.josseybass.com

Readers should be aware that Internet Web sites offered as citations and/or sources for further
information may have changed or disappeared between the time this was written and when it is read.

Limit of Liability/Disclaimer of Warranty: While the publisher and author have used their best efforts
in preparing this book, they make no representations or warranties with respect to the accuracy or
completeness of the contents of this book and specifically disclaim any implied warranties of
merchantability or fitness for a particular purpose. No warranty may be created or extended by sales
representatives or written sales materials. The advice and strategies contained herein may not be
suitable for your situation. You should consult with a professional where appropriate. Neither the
publisher nor author shall be liable for any loss of profit or any other commercial damages, including
but not limited to special, incidental, consequential, or other damages.

Jossey-Bass books and products are available through most bookstores. To contact Jossey-Bass directly
call our Customer Care Department within the U.S. at 800-956-7739, outside the U.S. at
317-572-3986, or fax 317-572-4002.

Jossey-Bass also publishes its books in a variety of electronic formats. Some content that appears in
print may not be available in electronic books.

Salesforce.com and the "No Software" logo are registered trademarks of salesforce.com, inc. Other
names may be marks of their respective holders.

Library of Congress Cataloging-in-Publication Data
Benioff, Marc R., 1964-
    Behind the cloud : the untold story of how Salesforce.com went from idea to billion-dollar
company—and revolutionized an industry / Marc R. Benioff, Carlye Adler. –1st ed.
        p. cm.
    Includes bibliographical references and index.
    ISBN 978-0-470-52116-8 (cloth)
    1. Salesforce.com (Firm) 2. Customer relations—Management. 3. Sales management. I. Adler,
Carlye. II. Title.
    HF5415.5.B443 2010
    658.8–dc22

                                                                                    2009021671

Printed in the United States of America
FIRST EDITION
HB Printing   20 19 18 17 16 15 14

Contents

CONTENTS

Contents

CONTENTS

Contents

For Lynne and the salesforce.com employees, customers, and investors—without whose unconditional support we would not be successful

Foreword

In 2001, in the midst of our previous economic meltdown, Marc Benioff came to me worried. Internet companies had evaporated overnight, and salesforce.com, a two-year-old company with a high proportion of dot-com customers, was ailing. "I'm scared about the future of my company," Marc said. "We can't get venture capital. I'm worried about survival."

It was a precarious time, but I knew then, as I know now, that economic shakeouts need not bode misfortune for technology companies. Not, at least, for innovative ones. Technology does not recognize economic recessions or depressions; it always continues. And, as all visionaries know, in chaos there is opportunity. I assured Marc that salesforce.com would last. "This is your time," I said. "You can do this."

I was bullish on salesforce.com and Marc, not because I have a crystal ball (though that certainly would be convenient), but because there was a need for change in the software industry and an audience ripening for salesforce.com's "End of Software" revolution. I had seen similar issues with affordability and accessibility plague the hardware industry when I started Dell.

Computers have long been a personal passion; growing up, I was fascinated with the machines but also struck by the inefficiencies in the industry, which required that we purchase computers from dealers, who bought them from distributors or manufacturers. Not only did that system yield a computer that cost four times the value of the parts inside, but it took so long that the machines were obsolete by the time customers got them. Buying direct from the source was an unprecedented idea in the industry, but it made common sense—even to a college student. The drive to implement simple new ideas and defy traditional ones has been the foundation of Dell—and the biggest reason our company has reaped huge rewards.

Salesforce.com sought to solve similar inefficiencies in the software industry. Enterprise software was exorbitantly expensive and onerous to implement, and, in the end, it didn't work very well. This was what enterprise customers came to expect. (Forget smaller customers; they couldn't even afford it.) Marc changed that reality when he used the Internet as a platform to deliver business software and reduce the risks and costs long associated with the client-server model. Saleforce.com made its service available to the masses, and it attentively and creatively engaged with its entire audience. It worked for the people who used the service (not only the folks paying for it), and it built what they requested. This earned salesforce.com an army of enthusiasts. And the company's focus on customer success forced all companies in the software industry—and far beyond—to rethink their models.

It certainly has inspired new thinking at Dell. Over the past few years, we committed to making some fundamental changes. We needed to refocus on providing the best customer experience, and we wanted to scale far beyond the commodity game and rapidly increase innovation. I went to Marc, who always seemed to be a machine for new ideas, and asked him, "How can we innovate faster?"

Marc told me about an internal networking technology they were using at salesforce.com to work with customers and create a "feedback loop." This discussion led to IdeaStorm, an online community forum that we now use to engage our customers, elicit their ideas, and help determine which ones to put into practice. The site, which is like a live 24/7 focus group, has helped field ideas from more than ten thousand customers and allowed us to offer better products, such as notebooks with Linux OS preinstalled, backlit keyboards, and computers with more USB ports. At the time I am writing this, our customers have contributed 11,289 ideas, which have been promoted by other customers more than 651,394 times, with over 84,908 comments. IdeaStorm enables us to listen as never before, and it was a turning point in restoring our reputation as a customer-centric company.

At Dell, we've seen the benefits of having Marc and salesforce.com on our side. It has helped us align twenty thousand members of our global sales team, integrate thousands of our global channel partners, and rapidly evolve ideas. That's why we're now deploying the service across Dell and putting it at the center of every customer interaction.

Eight years ago, Marc had concerns about salesforce.com's survival, but of course it didn't just survive—it thrived. It has earned the distinction as the first dot-com listed on the New York Stock Exchange, and today it generates more than $1 billion in annual revenue. Salesforce.com changed corporate philanthropy by integrating giving into its business model—and sharing that model so that myriad companies have collectively flooded talent, products, services, and billions of dollars into their communities. Because salesforce.com offers employees an opportunity to make a difference, not just earn a paycheck, it's known as one of the best places to work. Its original application has become the number-one hosted CRM service, and the company has established itself as the leader in the Software-as-a-Service (SaaS) industry it pioneered. And, through relentless focus, creativity, and passion, salesforce.com inspired an enterprise cloud computing industry. In short, the new and unconventional ideas that salesforce.com has evangelized have changed the way we do business and changed the world.

There has been a profound shift toward cloud computing in the past few years. Nearly every major public and private cloud is powered by Dell, and we are ecstatic to be running today's most exciting companies, including salesforce.com, Facebook, Microsoft, and many others. What motivates me most about this new way of computing is its potential for mass innovation. Now, for the first time, developers across the globe can access unlimited computing power. It's extraordinary that with a simple Web connection, anyone can build applications and deploy them to users everywhere.

By igniting the SaaS industry and then offering its Platform-as-a-Service, salesforce.com has spawned an ecosystem of countless new companies. It has offered large companies (such as Dell) and smaller companies just starting out valuable insights on how to innovate and succeed in the future.

In *Behind the Cloud*, Marc Benioff shares his unconventional advice in a clear and entertaining way. The lessons in this book are not exclusive to technology companies. They are applicable to all companies and all leaders who want to change the status quo and make a difference. Marc tells the inspiring story of how they did it at salesforce.com, and reveals how anyone else can, too. This is a great guide for any aspiring entrepreneur or CEO navigating the landscape of the future. It's the playbook for Enterprise 2.0.

We are in unprecedented economic times, but we are also in a new era of innovation. I tell anyone running a business today exactly what I told Marc when he was weathering a challenging climate: this is your time. You can do this. And, with the tools in this book, it will be easier and more rewarding than ever before.

Michael Dell
Founder, Chairman, and CEO of Dell

Introduction

This book is the story of how salesforce.com created a new industry, made our customers successful, and established itself as the market leader, all while making the world a better place. In this playbook, I'll share the strategies that I've developed during my thirty years in the technology business, the last ten as the cofounder and CEO of one of the fastest-growing software companies in the world.

I started salesforce.com in a rented apartment in 1999 with the goal of making enterprise software as easy to use as a Web site like Amazon.com. That idea—to deliver business applications as a service over the Internet—would change the way businesses use sophisticated software applications and, ultimately, change the way the software industry works. In less than a decade, our business has grown from a simple idea to a public company with more than a billion dollars in revenue.

We have achieved success by approaching business in a new way. The new models we have created—for marketing, sales, technology, finance, philanthropy, global expansion, and leadership—have been effectively employed by other companies, and we believe that any company can succeed with our strategies.

At a time when more entrepreneurs are starting companies faster and cheaper than ever before, the simple, accessible, and unconventional advice offered here will help you stand out, innovate better, and grow faster in any economic climate. The book follows the same easy-to-use and easy-to-implement mantras as our service. Divided into 111 "plays" (a fitting number, as our 1-1-1 model is so responsible for our success), it tells you how we developed award-winning breakthrough products, toppled much larger competitors, won customers of all sizes—and reveals how you can do all this too. As we promise customers who use our service, expect to see immediate results. That's not all, though. I'll show you how to build a business that's not just profitable but inspiring: good for your employees, good for your customers, and good for your community.

Perhaps like you, I have always wanted to be an entrepreneur. I grew up watching my father run a chain of women's clothing stores, and my grandfather, an innovative and unusual attorney, run his own practice and create BART, the San Francisco Bay Area Rapid Transit system. My obsession with software began when I wandered into a computer lab in high school. I would beg my grandmother to drive me to the local RadioShack so I could use the TRS 80 model 1. Later, I used the income I made at my after-school job (cleaning cases at a jewelry store) to buy my own computer. I wrote my first piece of software (How to Juggle) and sold it for $75.

What I really loved was the ways we could use computers to share information. When I was fifteen years old, I started my first company, Liberty Software, with some friends. We wrote adventure games for the Atari 800. My grandmother wrote the music for the games, and my parents were supportive of my entrepreneurial endeavors, even permitting me to travel to Europe on my own to research a castle I was going to replicate in a game. (The sense of independence that trip initially fostered was quelled when I forgot to phone home and my panicked mother called Scotland Yard. Embarrassing, but true.)

It was incredible to sell something that I had created from nothing. I took the reviews very seriously; even back then I knew that to be successful I needed to listen to the users. Luckily, the games did well. I was sixteen years old and earning royalties of about $1,500 a month. It was enough to buy a car and cover college.

I focused my studies at the University of Southern California on building companies and creating new technologies, and ran Liberty Software out of my dorm room. The lessons I learned as an entrepreneur were pivotal, as were those I learned working for somebody else. In 1984, I had a summer job at Apple writing some of the first native assembly language for the Macintosh. I had the opportunity to work on the most exciting and important project at Apple, and it was like getting paid to go to Disneyland. There were fruit smoothies in the refrigerators, a motorcycle in the lobby, and shiatsu massages.

The very best part was being able to witness Steve Jobs walking around, motivating the developers. Steve's leadership created the energy and spirit in the office. Apple encouraged the "think different" mind-set throughout its entire organization. We even had a pirate flag on the roof. That summer, I discovered that it was possible for an entrepreneur to encourage revolutionary ideas and foster a distinctive culture.

That lesson became even more obvious when I returned to Apple for a second summer internship as a technical sales support person with an Apple partner. Although only one year had passed, Apple was an extraordinarily different place. Steve Jobs had been fired, and everything I enjoyed about Apple's visionary culture had evaporated.

While the environment was not as invigorating, I learned another critical lesson that would guide the rest of my career: the power of each customer exchange. If the exchange was executed as well as possible—if we made the customer truly successful—we had the opportunity to transform him or her into an Apple loyalist and evangelist. This opened my eyes to the importance of customer success.

At heart I was still a shy computer programming geek addicted to building technology, but right before graduation, two of my entrepreneurship professors, Tom O'Malia and Mac Davis, offered some direct advice that significantly altered my path. They told me that the most successful business executives would be the ones who got real-world experience before starting their own companies. In their opinion, "real-world experience" was a sales position focused on building relationships with customers. They called it "carrying a bag."

Their advice led me to accept a job at Oracle, answering customer service calls that came into the software company's 800 number. I wasn't convinced that I wanted to dedicate myself to sales, and I didn't want to be an 800-number operator, but I soon discovered that working with customers was much more fun than writing code, and it turned out that I was pretty good at it.

Oracle had about two hundred people when I started, and the fast-growing company prized the efforts of young people and rewarded them. Founder and CEO Larry Ellison regularly walked the halls to chat with employees. (I usually took these opportunities to share my enthusiasm for Macs.) Soon after I sent Larry a note asking when Oracle would be on the Macintosh and included a business plan about how to make us successful in the Apple market, Larry made me the director of Oracle's Macintosh division.

Being responsible for the division that created software for personal computers was an amazing opportunity. Then, after Tom Siebel, the executive who ran direct marketing, resigned and recommended me as his replacement, I inherited an even more exciting and formative role.

It was Larry's vision that inspired me. He wanted me to create an "electronic village" and the next generation of sales and marketing using state-of-the-art electronic conferencing technology, software systems, and multimedia. Larry envisioned a world of interconnected computers that could easily share information across the planet at the touch of a button. The Internet seemed to offer a path to reach small and disaggregated customers, and I believed it could ultimately transform the industry.

By the mid-1990s, such companies as Amazon and Yahoo! were introducing a new way of life for consumers. Many of my colleagues were leaving Oracle to lead their own companies, most of which were traditional software plays. In many ways, Oracle served as an incubator where you got your legs, built a network of friends, and learned what you needed to go off on your own—and ultimately compete with Oracle. Although I had invested in several of these companies, I wasn't quite ready to leave Oracle University. I felt tethered to the growing corporation by the excitement of a powerful job and the security of a lucrative salary and addictive stock options. In addition, there was the relationship I had with Larry, my mentor and friend, one of the greatest software entrepreneurs in the industry's history. I was learning from the best.

During my tenure at Oracle, the company exploded into the second-largest software company in the world, right after Microsoft. Although its culture prized innovation, the company could no longer respond quickly or easily to new directions or opportunities. I found that limitation extremely challenging, and it eventually drove me to seek opportunities outside Oracle.

Maybe you are thinking about leaving a secure job to start your own company, or perhaps you are already running your own business. For me, launching salesforce.com was a way to respond to new directions and new opportunities that I could not pursue from inside an established corporation. It was a license to do things differently. From the very beginning, salesforce.com set out to build a new technology model (on-demand, or delivered over the Internet—now called cloud computing), a new sales model (subscription based), and a new philanthropic model (integrated into the corporation). Ten years later, we had succeeded on all of these fronts. We also had surpassed my expectations by creating the first $1 billion cloud computing company and spawning a new $46 billion industry, of which we are the market leader.

Read on to learn how we became one of the world's fastest-growing software companies and about the tremendous fun we've had along the way. You'll travel with us as we have our big entrepreneurial epiphany, as we turn a simple idea into a start-up company, and as we develop innovative technology and sell it through unconventional strategies. You'll witness our struggles, including coming close to bankruptcy during the dot-com disaster. Finally, you'll see how our unconventional ideas were validated through our listing on the New York Stock Exchange and how, through it all, we've found a way to give back.

The tactics and strategies that define our story can help any company succeed, and even become the next salesforce.com. So turn the page and envision your success. This is the first step in making it happen.

Behind
the Cloud

PART 1

The Start-Up Playbook
How to Turn a Simple Idea into a High-Growth Company

Play #1: Allow Yourself Time to Recharge

Some ideas hit with a big bang. Others take time to stew. The idea for salesforce.com had been simmering since 1996 when I was a senior vice president at Oracle. I had been there for ten years and was becoming something I had never anticipated: a corporate lifer.

I knew that I needed a change, but I wasn't sure what I wanted to do. Quit? Start a company? Take Oracle in a different direction? I was searching for balance in my life as well as an opportunity to pursue something meaningful. I took a badly needed sabbatical from work and rented a hut on the Big Island of Hawaii, where I enjoyed swimming with dolphins in the ocean and having enough time by myself to really think about the future.

My friends, including Oracle colleagues, came to visit. We had long talks about what the future would look like and what we wanted to do. Katrina and Terry Garnett were among those who spent time with me. Terry and I became friends when he ran marketing and business development for Oracle. He later moved to Venrock, the Rockefeller family's venture arm, celebrated for its wise investments in companies like Apple and Intel, and he was making investments in early-stage start-ups. I had a great respect for his market instincts. One day, during a swim, we began discussing online search engines and how the Internet was changing everything for consumers.

I was intrigued by Web sites such as Amazon.com, which revolutionized the way consumers shopped. I thought the Internet would change the landscape for businesses, too. I told Terry that I was exploring how to take the benefits of the consumer Web to the business world. He enthusiastically encouraged me to pursue my own Internet technology business. "You've been at Oracle forever; you know the safe route," he said. "But I think you are an entrepreneur. I think you can do something new."

After three months in Hawaii, I traveled to India for two months with Arjun Gupta, a good friend who was at a similar crossroads. We had an incredible awakening in India. One of our most invigorating meetings was with His Holiness the Dalai Lama, who talked about finding one's calling and the importance of community service. We also sought insight from the Hindu guru and humanitarian leader Sri Sri Ravi Shankar. But the most pivotal meeting for me was with Mata Amritanandamayi, commonly known as Ammachi, "the hugging saint," because she warmly embraces everyone who comes to visit her. She's hugged at least thirty million people and has calluses on her face from so many encounters. Known as the "mother of immortal bliss," she has dedicated her life to easing the suffering of others.

Arjun and I met privately with Ammachi, and it was she who introduced me to the idea, and possibility, of giving back to the world *while* pursuing my career ambitions. I realized that I didn't have to make a choice between doing business and doing good. I could align these two values and strive to succeed at both simultaneously. I told her I was thinking about leaving Oracle, and she told me, "Not yet."

My sabbatical was one of the most productive periods of my career; it was certainly one of the most influential. Don't be afraid to take time off when you need it. You could learn something that will change the course of your life, and at the least you will stave off the burnout that plagues so many driven, entrepreneurial people.

Play #2: Have a Big Dream

I saw an opportunity to deliver business software applications in a new way. My vision was to make software easier to purchase, simpler to use, and more democratic without the complexities of installation, maintenance, and constant upgrades. Rather than selling multimillion-dollar CD-ROM software packages that took six to eighteen months for companies to install and required hefty investments in hardware and networking, we would sell Software-as-a-Service through a model known as cloud computing. Companies could pay per-user, per-month fees for the services they used, and those services would be delivered to them immediately via the Internet, in the cloud.

If we hosted it ourselves and used the Internet as a delivery platform, customers wouldn't have to shut down their operations as their programs were installed. The software would be on a Web site that they could access from any device anywhere in the world, 24/7. This model made software similar to a utility, akin to paying a monthly electric bill. Why couldn't customers pay a monthly bill for a service that would run business applications whenever and wherever?

This delivery model seems so obvious now. Today we call it on-demand, Software-as-a-Service (SaaS), multitenant (shared infrastructure), or cloud computing. In fact, Nicholas Carr, former executive editor of the *Harvard Business Review* and one of the most influential thinkers in the IT industry, has since written two best-selling books validating this idea. Carr has even suggested that "utility-supplied" computing will have economic and social impacts as profound as the ones that took place one hundred years ago, when companies "stopped generating their own power with steam engines and dynamos and plugged into the newly built electric grid."[1]

The industry has come a long way, but consider that when we started, we didn't have these industry supporters, or even these words, to describe the computing revolution we believed was beginning. Although there was yet to be any kind of SaaS industry, I believed that all software would eventually be delivered in the cloud. I would soon find that in order to pursue my dream, I had to believe in it passionately and be ready to constantly defend it. This lesson learned during our earliest days still guides us today.

Play #3: Believe in Yourself

While I was in Hawaii, the customer relationship management (CRM) company Siebel Systems went public. I had worked with the founder, Tom Siebel, at Oracle, and was familiar with a sales force automation product called Oracle Automatic Sales and Information Systems (OASIS), which he had developed and had parlayed into Siebel. I thought a program that allowed salespeople to track leads, manage contacts, and keep tabs on account information was a great idea, and I had been an early angel investor in his company. Siebel took off, and the IPO netted me a great return, yet I also knew the product's flaws. This made me think about sales force automation (SFA) or CRM as an application category with revolutionary potential to be delivered on-demand, as a service.

SFA is a huge market; every company has some kind of sales force. In the late 1990s, when I was investigating the category, there was certainly room for improvement. Enterprise software was especially burdensome for the customer. It required maintenance and customization that needed months, or even years, to get right. It also required a hefty IT resource commitment, and more money than many companies wanted to spend on this aspect of their businesses. It struck me as curious that although this software was so troublesome, it remained wildly popular. I attributed this to the fact that if the software could increase sales productivity by even 5 percent, it made a meaningful difference to a business. What would happen, I wondered, if we offered a product that could increase productivity by the same amount, or more, *and* we made it easier to afford and use? Could you get a return on investment in six to twelve months rather than in three to five years? Replacing the traditional client-server model for an on-demand service that was simple and inexpensive seemed like a sure thing to me.

I had a number of conversations with Tom Siebel about creating an online CRM product. Typical licensing software was selling for extraordinary amounts of money. The low-end product could start around $1,500 per user per license. Worse, buying pricey software wasn't the only expense. There could be an additional $54,000 for support; $1,200,000 for customization and consulting; $385,000 for the basic hardware to run it; $100,000 for administrative personnel; and $30,000 in training. The total cost for 200 people to use a low-end product in the 1990s could exceed $1.8 million in the first year alone.[2]

Most egregious was that the majority of this expensive (and even more expensively managed) software became "shelfware," as 65 percent of Siebel licenses were never used, according to the research group Gartner.[3]

I told Tom about the SaaS CRM solution I envisioned. We would have "subscribers" pay a small monthly fee ($50 to $100, which added up to less than half the cost of the traditional systems), and we'd "operate" it so there would be no messy installation for the customer. Tom liked the idea so much that he invited me to join Siebel.

Through further discussions, however, I realized that Tom saw the potential only with the small business division, a tiny percentage of Siebel's market. I saw the idea as having much wider appeal. I thought it was something that could revolutionize the software industry. I knew Internet-based applications would eventually replace traditional offline software. I became passionate and obsessed with this idea, and decided to go after it on my own.

Play #4: Trust a Select Few with Your Idea and Listen to Their Advice

I was certain that I wanted to start salesforce.com, but I wasn't ready to openly discuss my idea. In fall 1998 I met for lunch with Bobby Yazdani, a friend from Oracle and the founder of the human capital management company Saba Software. We were getting together to discuss Saba, in which I had invested.

Like me, Bobby was struck by the transformation that was happening because of the Internet. We knew we were witnessing a major shift, and it wasn't long before our conversation turned to the subject of ambition and entrepreneurship.

"The number-one mistake entrepreneurs make is that they hold their ideas too closely to their chest," Bobby said. "Their destiny is their destiny, though. If they share their ideas, others can help make it happen."

I considered what Bobby was saying and silently acknowledged how I hadn't mentioned the idea of starting salesforce.com to anyone since Tom Siebel. Maybe Bobby had a valid point. I told him I wanted to build CRM online and deliver it as a service.

"It's very good you told me," he said.

"Why's that?"

"I have three men working for me as contractors. Not only do they have SFA experience, but they have experience with major Internet applications as well. They are the best of both worlds."

I couldn't believe this coincidence, or my good fortune. Bobby explained that the three developers had their own company, Left Coast Software, and that he had wanted to buy them out, but they weren't interested. They wanted to grow something, and felt that Saba was too far along. "They are brilliant engineers with good vision," Bobby said. "Let me introduce you to Parker Harris." I wasn't aware of it at the time, but by the end of that lunch my destiny was set.

Play #5: Pursue Top Talent as If Your Success Depended on It

I met with Parker Harris as soon as possible. "So, are you guys good?" I asked.

"We're some of the best people you'll find in the Valley."

I liked that confidence, especially considering that it was bolstered by what I had already heard. Still, I prepared myself for a very short meeting. Although Parker seemed like a promising technical candidate, I wasn't sure that this was the next move he had envisioned for himself. I'd heard that Parker had recently returned from a six-week trek in Nepal and told his business partners that he wanted to do something more meaningful than helping salespeople sell more. I was concerned that Parker would be fundamentally opposed to SFA and that he would think it boring because he had done it before.

I also thought that enterprise software was boring, but my vision was to do something much bigger. My vision was "the end of the software business and technology models" as we knew it. I believed that this was a great story and would appeal to Parker, who had majored in English literature at Middlebury College. Building this service also provided an intellectual challenge inasmuch as it had to be highly scalable, reliable, and secure; the service had to be something every customer could use simultaneously. I knew that the scaling test would be compelling to any great developer. I also had a trump card: Parker wanted to be in San Francisco. Every day, he endured a long commute from his house in the city to the Saba offices in Redwood Shores. "I have the same problem," I told him. "Salesforce.com will be in the city."

Parker was sold, but he had to get his business partners, especially the more pessimistic Dave Moellenhoff, to see the light.

Play #6: Sell Your Idea to Skeptics and Respond Calmly to Critics

On a Saturday morning in November 1998, the developers from Left Coast Software came to my house on Telegraph Hill to discuss building salesforce.com. I had written a short business plan in preparation for the meeting. After the developers read it, Dave told me all the reasons why it was "a crackpot idea" and would never work.

"It's an enterprise sale," Dave said.

"This is totally different than all of enterprise software. It's the next generation of companies that don't even sell software. It is a new, more democratic way. It is the end of the software technology model. It is the end of the software business model. It is the end of software as we know it," I replied.

"You'll have to invest a ton of time to land customers," Dave said. "Why would they trust this? Why would they buy this?"

"People want to be a part of something that is the future," I said. "Besides, people are frustrated with the current systems. This will be better: we'll deliver the applications as a Web site with easy-to-use tabs. It will be as simple as Amazon or Yahoo! Unlike our competitors, we're not asking for a big investment up front. The concept is a simple subscription model of $50 per user per month. It's 10 percent of what people are paying for Siebel—and, unlike Siebel, we'll have our customers forever."

"What about Siebel? Don't you find its dominance frightening?" asked Dave. "Is there room for someone else?"

"Siebel is unable to satisfy most companies out there. The Internet will allow us to give *all* companies an alternative solution for which they don't have to pay a fortune and that they will enjoy using. The Internet, with all this power and capability, will destroy the client-server companies that stand today. Technology is always becoming lower in cost and easier to use. It's a continuum. Let's ride it."

Dave tried to provoke me with negative comments about the products we built at Oracle (where I was still working). "Frankly, Oracle hasn't created anything great other than its database," he said.

I knew better than to take offense, and I simply disagreed politely. Later, Dave told me that he had planned to grill me to see how I would convince people of the concept and was also testing to see how I would react to negativity. He assumed that I must have had a temper to survive and thrive at Oracle—a Machiavellian environment perpetuated by Larry's well-known "management by ridicule" style. (It was no secret that insiders described the culture with the phrase "We eat our young.") That wasn't how I liked to operate, though. The time I'd spent in India and my commitment to practicing yoga and meditation served me well, as did reading Sun Tzu's *The Art of War*, which advocates keeping one's cool at all times.

How to Stay Calm in the Eye of the Storm

"He who is quick tempered can be insulted," Sun Tzu explained in the *Art of War*. These four checkpoints can help you stay cool — and retain your power — even in the most heated situations:

- Stay in the present moment.

- Observe your feelings. Do not become your feelings. Be aware of your reactions.

- Do not take on others' feelings, but listen to others — and yourself.

- Ask yourself, "How should I handle this? Should I react at all?"

Play #7: Define Your Values and Culture Up Front

On March 8, 1999, Parker Harris, Frank Dominguez, and Dave Moellenhoff began working in a one-bedroom apartment I'd rented at 1449 Montgomery, next door to my house. We didn't have office furniture, so we used card tables and folding chairs. What we lacked in furnishings, we made up for with an amazing view of the San Francisco Bay Bridge. I hung a picture of the Dalai Lama over the fireplace and another of Albert Einstein on the wall. Both were part of Apple's new ad campaign, and each said, "Think Different."

My summers at Apple had taught me that the secret to encouraging creativity and producing the best possible product was to keep people fulfilled and happy. I wanted the people who built salesforce.com to be inspired and to feel valued.

That wasn't to say there was anything glamorous about those early days. (The original server room was the bedroom closet, which also held Frank's clothes because he was flying down from Portland for the workweek and sleeping on a futon under his desk.) We built a culture simply by doing what we enjoyed. We wore Hawaiian shirts to instill the aloha spirit in the company. We ate late breakfasts at one of my favorite restaurants, Mama's, just down the street on Washington Square. Dave brought his dog to work. I got a dog too, a golden retriever named Koa, who also joined us in the office and soon got promoted to CLO (chief love officer).

Play #8: Work Only on What Is Important

We built the first prototype within a month. It didn't take very long because the developers knew sales force automation from their previous experiences. Further, it was a lot easier to build a Web site than to create complicated enterprise software. Our overarching goal was, as the developers said, to "do it fast, simple, and right the first time." The user interface was bare bones almost to a fault, but we wanted the service to be extremely easy to use. It had only the necessary information fields, such as contacts, accounts, and opportunities, which were initially organized by green tabs at the top of the screen. "No fluff," one of our first developers, Paul Nakada, used to say. Exactly like Amazon, I thought.

Our focus was directed at developing the best possible and easiest to use product, and this is where we invested our time. Realize that you won't be able to bring the same focus to everything in the beginning. There won't be enough people or enough hours in the day. So focus on the 20 percent that makes 80 percent of the difference.

Play #9: Listen to Your Prospective Customers

I invited friends and colleagues to visit the apartment, which I called the Laboratory, and asked them to test the prototype and offer feedback. Michelle Pohndorf Forbes, a family friend who was in sales, was one of the first people we invited to cycle through the prototype. She constantly reminded us to make the site easy to navigate with as few clicks as possible. My friends who worked at Cisco shared everything they hated about using traditional enterprise software products, and they walked us through what wasn't working for them. We listened and then responded by designing salesforce.com to be all the things that traditional software wasn't.

Unlike the way software had traditionally been developed—in secret—everyone was welcome at the Laboratory. When a group of Japanese businessmen were in town, they came to see what we were creating. We eventually became a stop on a tour for visiting Korean businesspeople who were interested in seeing an American start-up. Being inclusive of potential users from large and small companies across the world helped us gain valuable insight. After all, our goal was to build something that could serve as a global CRM solution for the masses.

In addition to asking dozens of people to cycle through the application, we hired Usability Sciences in Texas to test the product. The company provided feedback and videotapes of people using the site so that we could see what else needed tweaking. One problem we discovered, for example, was that our "create a new account" button was in the wrong place. It was on the right-hand side, and it disappeared on some monitors. By simply moving it to the left side, mirroring the way people read, we saw a huge improvement in the way people used the site. This experience proved the value of involving prospective users in order to build a user interface that was intuitive.

Play #10: Defy Convention

Asking users for feedback so that you can fine-tune a product or service to their needs is common sense. Yet this practice was completely counterintuitive to the way the software industry worked. Don't be afraid to ignore rules of your industry that have become obsolete or that defy common sense.

Creating an attractive user interface that people enjoy using is the key to building a truly great product. This seems so obvious, but it wasn't the way in which software design was customarily approached.

Steve Jobs is the master of building computer products that create customer excitement and loyalty. It's also no coincidence that his products look like nothing else out there. Think differently in everything you do.

Play #11: Have—and Listen to—a Trusted Mentor

When we first started building salesforce.com, I was still working at Oracle, where I was creating a new software product called Internet File System and developing the company's philanthropy program. I had many long conversations with my boss, Larry

Ellison, about my outside endeavor. Brainstorming with Larry about new ideas and products had always been the best part of my job, and Larry was very insightful and encouraging when it came to salesforce.com. He gave me permission to work at salesforce.com in the mornings and come to Oracle in the afternoons. I was grateful for that unusual arrangement.

Then, after I'd been running and self-financing salesforce.com for ninety days, Larry suggested I take a leave of absence from Oracle. He said that if salesforce.com didn't work out, I could come back—a remarkable and generous offer. Larry valued loyalty, and until that time, he'd been quick to say "good riddance" to anyone who expressed an interest in moving beyond Oracle. Larry was much more than my boss, though. He was my mentor for more than a decade as well as a close friend.

Throughout the thirteen years we worked together, Larry and I spent countless hours discussing potential future innovations. Larry believed that salesforce.com was the next big idea, and he invested $2 million in seed money and joined the board of directors. He knew that I needed top talent, and as he was aware that Oracle would be the first place I would look to find it, he requested I take only three people from Oracle with me to salesforce.com.

Play #12: Hire the Best Players You Know

I obliged Larry's request to limit my use of Oracle as a recruiting fair, but I was ecstatic about the opportunity to handpick three talented and well-trained individuals to help build salesforce.com. I asked Nancy Connery to run recruiting and human resources, something we desperately needed. I tapped

The Larry Ellison Playbook

Many of the lessons I learned from Larry still guide me today. Most of all, he taught me that accomplishments are fueled by faith. When Oracle entered its darkest days, every employee, customer, analyst, and even the people closest to him doubted the company would rebound. Even in that difficult climate, Larry's resolve never faltered. What I learned from Larry:

- Always have a vision.
- Be passionate.
- Act confident, even when you're not.

Jim Cavalieri to build the hardware on which the software would run. Jim didn't know anything about sales force automation, as his background was large databases, but I believed he could build a system with the right infrastructure that would allow us to scale to support millions of users. Later I hired Mitch Wallace, whom I had also met at Oracle. I had been impressed by the inventiveness Mitch showed in building an application for the California Mentor Initiative, and he had been a key player in helping me build Oracle's philanthropy program.

Thanks to Nancy's focus on hiring, we began to grow, and our burgeoning team soon took over the entire apartment. I based the developers in the Laboratory, which was upstairs, with the view, and moved the marketing and salespeople, aka the "talkers," downstairs so that they wouldn't distract the engineers. (Engineers rule.) Eventually, I banned the talkers from the upstairs entirely in order to maintain a serene environment for the developers. We used the balcony as the conference room.

- Think of it as you *want* it, not as it is!

- Don't let others sway you from your point of view.

- See things in the present, even if they are in the future. (We joked that Larry got his tenses confused because he would talk about things that hadn't happened yet as if they had. This taught me that a successful leader is one who is always thinking about the future, not just the present. Wayne Gretzky famously put it another way: "Skate to where the puck is going, not where it has been.")

- Don't give others your power. Ever.

Our friend Jim Gray, the legendary computer scientist and head of Microsoft research, who was tragically lost at sea in 2007, was nearby as well. He sent me an e-mail in 1999 asking what I was doing. When I told him, he replied, "There goes the neighborhood."

In a way, Jim Gray was right. It wasn't long before our growing staff appropriated my house next door. The developers strung Ethernet cable out the office window, through the redwood trees, and into my home so that we could all communicate. (These were the dark days before wireless.) My assistant worked from my home, as did Nancy, who ran human resources in a downstairs bedroom with a product manager, a business development manager, and a part-time attorney. It wasn't ideal. I would often come downstairs to get breakfast and find recruits sitting on my living room sofa. As we were growing into a real company with an amazing and dedicated team, salesforce.com was quickly filling every corner of my life.

Play #13: Be Willing to Take a Risk—No Hedging

A few months into building salesforce.com, Magdalena Yesil, a fellow entrepreneur and salesforce.com's first investor, and I were leaving a promising meeting with a potential investor when she turned to me and said, "The next major step is for you to fully leave Oracle and end your leave of absence. It is time to be a full-time entrepreneur."

This caught me by surprise. I had assumed that I could nurture salesforce.com without abandoning Oracle. I had spent so much of my career at Oracle, and it had become so much a part of my identity. I realized that Magdalena was right, though. It was time to cut my other ties and devote everything I had to building salesforce.com. After all, I was relentlessly passionate about the idea, which made me willing to take an enormous risk. This was a major turning point in how I viewed the company and my role in it.

In July 1999, salesforce.com became my full-time job. The first decision I made was that having everyone working next door and out of my living room was not the most sustainable solution. On my first official full day of work, I went out to look for new office space. My sister's friend recommended the Rincon Center. I liked it immediately because there were dolphins decorating the building, and I viewed this as a positive sign because I had developed the idea for salesforce.com while swimming with dolphins in Hawaii. Parker and the team came to see the new space. It was nearly eight thousand square feet and long and narrow. At the time, there were ten employees at salesforce.com. "That's way too much space," Parker said.

How to Leave a Place Where You Have Invested Everything—Without Burning Bridges

Leaving the comfort and security of a current position to start your own venture is exciting—and daunting. You'll first need to do your own soul-searching to gain the necessary confidence. These five tips can help make the process of leaving easier, and ultimately make the venture more successful.

Seek the encouragement and support of your mentor. The best mentors encourage their mentees to take risks and push their limits. These mentors will serve as an important support system.

Build a welcoming environment with familiar faces. At salesforce.com, we initially hired people from our own circles—be it from our social circles, fellow alumni from Oracle, or even from college. Using this approach made it easy for me to feel fully confident in my team, and made our first employees—people who also left secure roles—feel more comfortable and excited about embarking on this adventure.

Embrace increased responsibility. The opportunity to grow your career is always a key reason to make a move from a secure company.

Consider the thrill of the unknown. Joining a start-up is one of life's most exciting and rewarding experiences. Sure, it has its ups and downs like a ride at an amusement park, but for many people that's enjoyable.

Weigh the ability to take risks. Having faith in your abilities is essential, but so is examining where you are in life and whether or not risk-taking is an option.

"We'll never use it all. What are you doing?" He was very upset and concerned.

I wasn't thinking about the company we were at that moment. I was thinking about the company I wanted us to be. "I like it; we're going to take it." I said. "We'll be out of here before you know it." Parker did not believe me.

Play #14: Think Bigger

In summer 1999 we had ten employees and a two-page Web site (a home page and a recruiting page requesting that resumes be sent to cooljobs@salesforce.com). Everywhere we looked, Internet companies were growing wildly, and financial deals were heating up. We were constantly talking about the deals of the past few years, such as Hotmail, which had sold for $400 million.

"That's a lot of money, Marc. Don't you think that's a lot of money?" asked Frank Dominguez, one of the salesforce.com developers and cofounders, referring to the Hotmail deal.

"No, I would never sell for that. They left a lot of money on the table," I replied. Frank couldn't believe that I could think so big when we were still so small. Although the other founders were initially leery about our move to the Rincon Center, they quickly grew to like the new larger space. They drove golf balls down the length of the office and flew remote-control helium blimps. We had no office furniture, so we put tables by the outlets that were already there. Everyone had to set up his or her own desks (we bought sawhorses and doors at Home Depot), and employees received their computers in boxes and put them together themselves. It was an archetypal California start-up scene with a dog in the office and a mass of young and energetic people wearing Hawaiian shirts, working hard, and subsisting on pretzels, Red Vines licorice, and beef jerky.

In typical dot-com style, we exploded. By the time cofounder Dave Moellenhoff returned from his three-week honeymoon in November 1999, the staff had doubled. As I had promised Parker, about one year after we moved into the Rincon Center, we were bursting out of the space. Three salespeople had desks in a hallway, and five IT specialists had taken over the conference room. Our next move, in November 2000, was to shiny new offices at One Market Street. It was only a block away, so we put the servers on office chairs and rolled them across the street. Although we were not going any great distance geographically, the leap ushered in an entirely new era for our company.

PART 2

The Marketing Playbook
How to Cut Through the Noise and Pitch the Bigger Picture

Play #15: Position Yourself

Even before salesforce.com officially launched, we understood the value of a marketing-obsessed culture, and we strove to generate excitement about our new on-demand delivery model. Don Clark, a reporter at the *Wall Street Journal*, visited us while we were still based in the apartment, and he wrote a front-page story called "Canceled Programs: Software Is Becoming an Online Service, Shaking Up an Industry." Published on July 21, 1999, the article illustrated the shift that was occurring. Clark cited our company, founded only six months before, as one of the examples. He wrote that I was "driven by a chance to make high-tech history," and he closed the article by quoting me saying, "This will be the spawning of a new industry."[1]

The article helped us position ourselves as we had wanted (as revolutionaries) and made me realize that we were in the public arena. We needed a real Web site. Immediately. I asked Parker Harris to build it overnight, and that turned out to be an auspicious decision. We received five hundred leads the next day! It became clear that we were truly on to something.

We continued to unveil our idea to beta customers, and that fall, I went to Monaco to attend the European Technology Roundtable Exhibition (ETRE), the world's most influential gathering of technology CEOs. At the time, we did not have a public relations agency to help us garner press. Although I had wanted to engage OutCast Communications, a firm with which I had worked on a project at Oracle, founder Caryn Marooney was too busy to start work for us right away. Luckily, Pam Alexander, a noted high-tech strategist, found me at the ETRE show and convinced me to have a press party. I hosted a small party in my suite at the beautiful Hôtel de Paris, and I demonstrated the product to a group of thirty people.

Pam was correct in her assumption that the industry would be interested in hearing from us. Prominent journalists attended, including David Kirkpatrick of *Fortune* and David Einstein, the West Coast bureau chief of *Forbes*, and people understood that we were talking about something bigger than CRM: "The End of Software."

We began to get more exciting press activity, mostly online at first. I believe that the coverage opened Caryn's eyes that we had something important to say, and OutCast Communications took us on as a client. Having the right agency would be pivotal to our image and success.

Whether or not you engage a PR firm, always ask yourself, "What's my message?" Position yourself either as the leader or against the leader in your industry. Every experience you give a journalist or potential customer must explain why you are different and incorporate a clear call to action. This does not require a large team or a big budget; it just requires your time and focus.

Play #16: Party with a Purpose

As the calendar flipped from 1999 to 2000, we readied ourselves to introduce salesforce.com to the world properly and officially. This was the era of the extravagant dot-com bash (one company hired performers from Cirque du Soleil; another flew in an accordion player from Turkey).[2] Even against this backdrop of excess, I wanted the salesforce.com launch to stand out.

We held our event at San Francisco's Regency Theater. Although we wanted our guests to enjoy the party and planned the menu and entertainment to ensure that they did, the event also carried a much larger mission. Unlike other dot-com parties, which functioned to introduce a company and its products, we needed to introduce an entirely new market (on-demand, or SaaS, or cloud computing) and promote a new way of doing business.

Salesforce.com used this difference to its advantage and created a story about waging war against the traditional and ineffective way software was delivered. Our mission was to offer a new and better way to serve customers. This story would be the keystone of our entire business. I believed that if we took our customers' view—and figured out how to make them successful—we would be profitable. This approach might sound like common sense now, but at the time it was completely contrarian to the established model.

We hired the B-52s, the "world's greatest party band," which made for lively and unique entertainment. To tell our story, we transformed the lowest level of the theater into a space that represented enterprise software, aka hell. There were cages with actors playing captured enterprise salespeople locked inside. "Help, get me out," they screamed. "Sign this million-dollar license agreement. I need to make my quota!" There were carnival games, including Pitch CDs in the Toilet and Whack-a-Mole, where the moles to be whacked were other software company logos.

After our guests worked their way through this inferno, they progressed to limbo. Finally, when they were ready, they were able to go up one more level and obtain Nirvana. The top floor represented heaven. There was a harp. There was light. There was salesforce.com.

At a cost of about $600,000 (the B-52s were $250,000 alone), the event wasn't inexpensive, but it drew more than fifteen hundred attendees and earned us a firestorm of invaluable press. Most important, the audience and the press remembered the story of change we were disseminating.

At the time of the party, we had a small amount of revenue and were not profitable. I wasn't concerned about that, but not because this was during the go-go days marked by the "profits don't matter" mind-set. I was confident that salesforce.com would be very profitable. In order to get there, though, we needed to build a powerful brand behind our great service. There wasn't time to waste; companies must embrace bold marketing tactics from the beginning in order to break through all the industry noise.

I stood up at the party and made a daring comment, but one that I believed wholeheartedly: "We are going to be a $100 million company three years from now," I declared. "We're going to be the last dot-com."

A few weeks after the party, the NASDAQ hit its peak of 5,048. Dot-coms were flying higher than ever. Then, only a few months later, almost all of them came crashing down. As the dot-com rush panned mostly fool's gold, many critics and colleagues wondered aloud about the future of salesforce.com. People suggested we drop the "dot-com" from our name, as the whole category was being branded "dot-bombs" or "dot-cons." I never considered it. I still believed in the power of the Internet to change everything. And as any entrepreneur would agree, failure was not an option.

Play #17: Create a Persona

I played the role of revolutionary at our launch party and even wore army fatigues because I needed to demonstrate that I was ready to lead our battle against the established software industry. This readiness to fight for what we believed represented the vision and values of our company. As the founder of this mission, it was my job to walk the talk.

Many CEOs are leery of getting too personal and are wary of inventing a mythical persona. Don't be afraid to step into the forefront and take risks. Most of the world's best CEOs are indistinguishable from the companies they run. Embracing a "role" establishes them as thought leaders and gives them a certain celebrity status that begets invitations to speak with the press, at events, and on panels—prime opportunities to spread their messages.

Anyone can create a persona, but it takes time and energy to do it properly. Your "character" must fit with your company's story to bolster your brand. It must be heartfelt and authentic to who you are if it is to be successful. It should not be mere artifice.

People seem to think this is difficult, or even impossible for somebody who is more reserved. That's not the case. Anyone can do this, especially because it doesn't require that you immediately accept a new part. I wasn't wearing fatigues on our first day; the idea emerged months into building salesforce.com, after we developed our mission and honed our message. Learn and build as you go and allow your persona to develop.

Play #18: Differentiate, Differentiate, Differentiate

When starting any new initiative, I like to seek the insight of the brightest minds. My "go to the guru" approach led me to hire Bruce Campbell to help brand salesforce.com. Bruce is one of the best admen in the business. He branded and launched Saturn, was part of the "Tuesday Team" for President Reagan's Morning in America TV campaign, and helped in rebranding public television, Bank of America, and the Gallo Winery. I shared with him our "End of Software" mission, and he came to me with an idea for a NO SOFTWARE logo (the word SOFTWARE in a red circle with a line though it; think Ghostbusters). It was perfect. It was simple. It was sexy. It was fun. I especially liked that it fit on a button. I also appreciated the phone number it inspired, 1-800-NO-SOFTWARE, which provided customers an easy way to find us.

Although I loved the NO SOFTWARE logo immediately, almost everyone else hated it. It was important to find out everyone's reasoning, and my trusted advisers made some valid points. "It violates the number-one rule of marketing: never promote yourself with a negative message," our PR team explained. Others were concerned that we would alienate customers. As they pointed out, many of our customers were software companies. Further, members of the press tended to get bogged down in semantics. "It's not accurate," they said. "You still make software; you just deliver it differently."

Given these concerns, even the people on the salesforce.com team believed that moving forward with this slogan and logo was a disastrous idea. In fact, the staff tried to ignore it, hoping that it would disappear. Although research and logic were behind some of their concerns, I felt that their arguments were overruled by the most important rule in marketing—the necessity to differentiate your brand. Our differentiators were ease of use, a business model of shared risk, and low-risk commitment—everything that software was not.

The End of Software mission and the NO SOFTWARE logo effectively conveyed how we were different. I put the logo on all our communications materials and policed it to make sure no one removed it. (They did so anyway.) I wore a NO SOFTWARE button every day and asked our employees to as well. (They did so, somewhat reluctantly.) It wasn't just the logo that we used to gain recognition. The dot-com in our name and our gonzo PR strategies (more on those later) were also tactics that served our differentiation strategy.

In an effort to further raise the collective consciousness about our war against software, I created a provocative advertisement with a fighter jet shooting a biplane. The fighter jet represented our company, which was built on the most advanced technology and was a vast improvement on anything that came before it. The biplane was a metaphor for the software industry: obsolete and ill-suited for its task.

The inside story is that I stole this entire concept from Larry Ellison and Oracle. Previously, Larry had commissioned an advertisement with Oracle as the fighter plane taking down its database competitors, which were depicted (you guessed it) as biplanes. I knew that an updated version would pay homage to my origins and serve as the perfect vehicle to introduce our cutting-edge End of Software campaign. After receiving permission from Rick Bennett, the advertising genius behind the Oracle ad, I hired the same artist Oracle had used, to create an illustration for us. Our advertising agency thought the illustration was silly, but I had previously seen it effectively convey an important message. With a hunch that it could succeed again, I turned it into an advertisement for salesforce.com.

I showed the ad to Michael Liedtke and Jessica Guynn, reporters at the *Contra Costa Times*, who wrote a spirited weekly business column called "Synergize This." They immediately appreciated the concept and understood that we were a different kind of company on a mission to disrupt the way things were done.

It was a surprise even to me, however, when the *Times* ran the advertisement as art on the front page of the business section along with an editorial feature on salesforce.com and The End of Software revolution. The newspaper included the entire color advertisement without our having to pay a cent for it! It was a coup in the ad business and a major triumph for our company. Bruce Campbell couldn't believe it. He had thought the fighter jet ad was ridiculous. Imagine his surprise when the *Contra Costa Times*, his hometown paper, was delivered that morning! All of this made me very happy: we proved that differentiating ourselves was a powerful marketing strategy that worked. (As far as the particulars are concerned, if the press loves it, so do I.)

The epilogue to this story is that the ad did run as an advertisement in the *Wall Street Journal*, and its audacity drew even more attention to salesforce.com. The part I find most amusing is that no one except for Larry (and Rick Bennett) knew that I had stolen the concept from Oracle. Essentially, this was my way of bowing to Larry, who had taught me a tremendous amount. By allowing me to do this, Larry confirmed that he was truly my mentor, someone who encouraged me to take what I learned from him and elevate it to new heights.

A Brand Is Not Just a Logo—It's Your Most Important Asset

I love the NO SOFTWARE logo; it's not our brand, though. "A logo is simply a graphic representation of a company," says Bruce Campbell, the creator of the logo and our chief creative officer. "A brand is more. It has to be a collective set of memories."

To be effective, a company's brand must be consistent. A company must use its people, its products, and its messaging to consistently reinforce the same positive points it wants to demonstrate. A delivery service that promises to meticulously care about your packages cannot have dirty trucks. A bank that says it cares about its customers can't have twenty people waiting in line with only two tellers on duty. Brands cannot break the promises they make. Broken promises destroy customers' trust. That ruins everything.

A brand is a company's most important asset. A company can't "own" its facts. If the company's facts (speed, price, quality) are superior to the competition, any good competitor will duplicate them, or worse, improve upon them, as soon as possible. What a company *can* own, however, is a personality. We own NO SOFTWARE — not because we are the only one doing it but because we were the first to think it was important to customers. By consistently delivering an attitude that is future focused and pioneering, we have created a personality. We act the way people expect us to, which has made them feel connected to us. It goes beyond logic. It's an emotional attachment, and that's an asset that cannot be stolen by any competitor.

Play #19: Make Every Employee a Key Player on the Marketing Team, and Ensure Everyone Is On Message

One day, early in our occupancy at the Rincon Center, our marketing director, a developer, a quality assurance person, and an engineer were in the elevator when another tenant in the building asked, "What exactly does salesforce.com do?" To my surprise, everybody gave a different answer.

This was troublesome. Everyone at our company needed to understand who we were and what we did. More important, they needed to be able to effectively relay it in one simple sentence to anybody who asked and everybody who would listen. Because that consistent message clearly hadn't made its way to our employees on its own, we had to educate them. This presented an amazing opportunity: if we succeeded, we could transform every employee into a marketing representative.

To ensure that everyone was on the same page (literally), our PR firm, OutCast Communications, produced a two-sided laminated card. It was a marketing cheat sheet that stated in one sentence what we did. It also provided information about the benefits of our service, our newest customers and partners, and our most recent awards. With this card, we leveraged everyone—from developers to engineers to quality assurance people—as integral parts of our marketing organization.

The card would have been of little use if we had simply distributed it. Instead, we offered training to make sure that everyone was crystal clear on the message that we wanted delivered to the world. In the early days, we met with the whole company for brown-bag lunch sessions to go over the latest marketing pitch for the company. Even though we were small, it was essential to ensure that our marketing was focused and first class.

Over time, as we grew, we required that all customer-facing employees become "certified" in how to position the service and how to deliver our messages. We taught everyone how to defend the messages against objections, which made them feel more prepared and confident. One of the more unusual aspects of our pitches is that we made them "role based," meaning that we would present a different problem-solving solution angle to a CIO than we would to a sales manager. The ultimate result of this meticulous coordination is that everyone is on message with the precision of a sophisticated political campaign.

Play #20: Always, Always Go After Goliath

We routinely updated the card to reflect our current customers and partners, but there was always one item that stayed the same: our competitor. Salesforce.com only acknowledged one competitor—the market leader. After all, that was the only position for which we were vying. Furthermore, it cast us in the right role as the underdog and the visionary. It's always wise to play the visionary card. Everyone roots for you. If there is no Goliath in your industry, go after the status quo.

Although we wanted to position ourselves against Goliath, we hadn't always planned to attack our much larger competitor directly. In a way, that started by accident. February 22, 2000, the day of The End of Software salesforce.com launch party, was also the day of a giant Siebel User Group conference in downtown San Francisco. This coincidence was truly unplanned,

Is Everyone in Your Organization On Message?

First, take the time to answer the questions here. Your responses are what will determine how your company will be viewed by the outside world.

Invite your team to fill out the answers to these questions. If you see varied responses, it's time to get everyone in alignment. Create your own "cheat sheet" card and distribute it throughout the organization.

What we are:

(What do we want?)

_____

Benefits:

(What is important to customers about what we do?)

_____

Customers:

(What are our most successful customer stories?)

_____

Key partners:

(What makes them successful using our product?)

_____

Competitors:

(How are we different from our competitors?)

_____

but once we discovered it, we decided to use the flurry of activity around Siebel's event to our advantage.

On the morning of the conference, we sent protesters (in reality, paid actors) to the Moscone Center to picket the conference. They waved mock protest signs—NO SOFTWARE posters—and shouted, "The Internet is really neat ... Software is obsolete!" We also hired actors to pretend to be a TV crew from local station KNMS, who came on location to cover The End of Software movement. "What do you think of the Internet?," a fake TV reporter asked passersby, pointing a microphone toward them. I had originally planned to have a tank roll in with someone dressed as General Patton, but later decided that such a stunt might be too outlandish. Even without the general, we won the interest of conference attendees. We also captured the attention of the competition. Twenty Siebel executives poured out of Moscone to investigate. A Siebel executive called the police, who immediately arrived to protect the protesters!

The police presence only fanned the flames. The resulting hullabaloo helped attract an even larger audience, and the police couldn't stop our mock protest because we were there legally. It was exciting to plan this attack, and the marketing team enjoyed watching the scene unfold from a stakeout car, but this effort had a higher purpose than having a good time at the competition's expense. We approached every person who went into the Siebel conference and gave him or her an invitation to the salesforce.com launch party that night. (Many of them showed up!)

This marketing stunt worked across many fronts: we built salesforce.com morale, got great press coverage, and brought our competitor's customers to our event to hear our message. Within two weeks, more than one thousand organizations signed up for our service; most were introduced to it through articles about the launch. Later, our End of Software campaign was recognized by *PR Week* as the "Hi-Tech Campaign of the Year." We would use this type of creative approach to attack the competition many more times.

Play #21: Tactics Dictate Strategy

One idea alone is a tactic, but if it can be executed a number of different ways, it becomes a great strategy. Because the guerilla tactic of directly leveraging the activities of our competition worked so well, we repeated it and made it one of our marketing strategies. I learned this idea from the marketing classic *Positioning: The Battle for Your Mind*, by Al Ries and Jack Trout.

Everyone at salesforce.com constantly brainstormed about opportunities to leverage our competition's activities for our own benefit. One of my favorite examples was when we found a way to use a Siebel conference in San Diego as a prime platform for our then-new "wake up and smell the salesforce.com coffee" success messaging.

On the day of the conference, right in time for the morning rush, Elizabeth Pinkham, senior vice president who runs our events, gathered a crew of temps on bicycle rickshaws outside the San Diego Convention Center. They offered rides to the two thousand conference attendees and handed out free Krispy Kreme doughnuts and Peet's coffee in mugs that cited a great analyst quote, "Wake up Siebel, salesforce.com is a disruptive technology and is slowly moving in on the CRM prize." (US Bancorp, Piper Jaffray) That wasn't all. We gave Siebel customers salesforce.com marketing materials with quotes from recent press articles, and during the rickshaw rides we had the chance to speak with them about the benefits of the salesforce.com service. The fun spirit we created sparked the interest of even the biggest Siebel devotees, and many brought salesforce.com-branded mugs (and talking points) into the conference. Even Tom Siebel graciously accepted a cup of coffee.

Later, we devised a way to transfer attention from the competition to our company at Siebel's European User Week. The conference was in Cannes, France, which most visitors access by flying into Nice and taking an airport taxi to Cannes. We rented all the taxis and used the forty-five-minute drive, which we provided for free, as an opportunity to pitch our service. We decorated the vehicles with NO SOFTWARE logos and filled them with our marketing brochures. The executives, left with no other option than to take our rides, became irate and called the police (again).

We succeeded because we caught our competitor by complete surprise. (This was another tactic I learned from *The Art of War*, in which Sun Tzu advises, "appear at places where he must rush to defend, and rush to places where he least expects.") Participating in our competitor's events helped us weave our name into its stories, articles we knew would garner a lot of attention. To further leverage its announcements, we issued press releases about salesforce.com's new features or new customers the same day its quarterly earnings releases went live. We meticulously planned so that anyone looking for Siebel always found salesforce.com. Eventually, when anyone thought about Siebel, he or she also thought about salesforce.com. The reality was that we were still the gnat on the back of an elephant, but our unusual tactics were making that elephant dance.

Play #22: **Engage the Market Leader**

We were always looking for new ways to differentiate ourselves, and we began considering an ad campaign that would directly take on the competition. I called Rick Bennett, who had done the biplane ad, and he came up with "Don't get bullied," a campaign featuring a schoolboy writing on a chalkboard. One advertisement showed the schoolboy (my cousin) writing the message, "I will not give my lunch money to Siebel" one hundred times. Another had him writing, "I will not spend my summer vacation installing Siebel."

The attack ads put our adversary's executives in a quandary. To comment would be to acknowledge us as a viable competitor. It wasn't long, though, before Siebel began to react. "There's no way that company exists in a year," Tom said of salesforce.com in an interview with *Fortune*. In response to the *Wall Street Journal* running our ad, Tom later commented, "I am surprised that any reputable publication would agree to run an ad of such questionable taste."[3] Although I don't think that its executives ever understood this, the fracas with Siebel was not personal. We had a problem with the traditional software model that didn't care about customers' success. We believed that "business as service," pursuing long-term customer engagement, was better for our bottom line.

There is a Japanese belief that business is temporal, whereas relationships are eternal. That's true. One day you compete. The next day you partner. One day someone is your subordinate; the next day he or she may be your superior. At its finest, business is friendly competition, just like a game of tennis.

As I was hitting balls over the net, the competition should have been hitting balls back at me. Instead, whenever we pulled off some guerilla PR tactic or beat Siebel to an account or lured over one of its executives, people at the company took it personally. That emotional reaction put the company at a disadvantage. Don't ever let the competition make you angry. You must have clarity of mind to make your own decisions—not the ones that your competitors want you to make. You must be transparent to the competition. See, recognize, and understand what your competitor is doing.

Siebel executives did not see what was obvious (that we were trying to rattle them), and as the company began defending itself and acknowledging salesforce.com, we chipped into its airtime. The press began to see this fight as an increasingly interesting story, and that further legitimized us. The tail started to wag the dog. At this point, we had already won.

Play #23: Reporters Are Writers; Tell Them a Story

Although the battle between salesforce.com and Siebel wasn't driven by a personal feud, the press didn't see it that way, and reporters loved building drama around this story. That makes sense. After all, reporters like to tell a story with a protagonist and a villain.

It was fortuitous that journalists already saw Siebel as the villain. At user conferences, Siebel irked reporters by separating them from everyone else and leading them around like sheep. Salesforce.com, in contrast, welcomed journalists, encouraged them to mix with customers at events, and eagerly introduced them to customers for interviews. "Talk to whomever you want," we said. As customers shared stories of their successes with salesforce.com and this new model, we differentiated ourselves and emerged as the little upstart that could. The press became our best ally.

The reality was that in terms of revenue and customers, we were still just a tiny little start-up. No one at the *Wall Street Journal*, the *New York Times*, or *BusinessWeek* really cared about a small start-up. However, they did care about a small start-up that pledged to upend the industry leader. Journalists welcomed hearing from a challenger that was a harbinger of an industry-wide transformation.

Being an agent of change was a key element of our marketing strategy. A David versus Goliath story is interesting, but we had to pitch the bigger picture. That's where The End of Software story came in. We painted a picture that showed that the industry was changing. We talked about what our competitors did wrong. We introduced our solution. We explained why it was good for customers. We talked about the future and tapped into the large audience of people who cared about what would happen next.

Play #24: Cultivate Relationships with Select Journalists

I enjoy meeting with journalists. As an author and someone who prizes communication as the most essential part of my job, I also identify with them. Even while I appreciate the conversations I have with these professionals who care about what they are observing in the world and who are constantly thinking about the future, I also consider my relationships with journalists and bloggers to be a pivotal part of our marketing strategy.

I never treat members of the media as adversaries; they are friends of the company. I keep a list of about two dozen reporters whom I consider influential worldwide, and I pay extra special attention to them. I maintain my relationships with these individuals through in-person meetings and frequent contact. I ensure that it is simple for them to reach me. They have my direct contact information and do not have to go through our PR department to connect with me. I continually keep in touch by sending them information that I think would be helpful to them.

Developing these relationships has provided tremendous opportunities. Journalists immediately think of me as a resource for a quote or comment because they know that I will be available to offer fresh insight and meet their deadlines. Relationships engender trust so that when I send out a memo or comment, these journalists are more receptive to it. For example, when I heard that Microsoft (finally) announced that it wanted to enter the SaaS business with a CRM product, I fired off an e-mail to select journalists: "Well, it's 7:29 A.M. in Singapore, and I just read that Microsoft announced a new offering to compete with us while I was asleep." I included the interoffice memo that I had written (I'd done this before; tactics dictate strategy), and the *San Francisco Chronicle* ran an article about my response on its Web site. They included what I said in the e-mail and even reiterated their "favorite line" of the memo: "Steve Ballmer has publicly fretted that he would not be 'out-hustled by anyone,' but the fact is that Microsoft is being out-hustled by everyone." Even better, they ran the entire memo in another section. No doubt, sending carefully chosen members of the press well-crafted office memos is one more way to get your story told.

A large part of our marketing and PR strategy is making sure that we always remain relevant. One of the ways we do this is by making ourselves available to discuss the direction of the industry. We don't just sit around and wait for someone to call. If something happens that I can leverage, I immediately send a journalist an e-mail with my comments or "leak" an internal memo. I also like to forward related articles and other people's ideas that help establish our point. For instance, we often referenced Clayton M. Christensen's *The Innovator's Dilemma* and Nicholas Carr's *The Big Switch*, two thought-provoking books that validated our crusade.

It is essential to spend time learning about what is happening in your industry to leverage these opportunities as well as to prevent being caught off guard. Using industry news to our advantage has served us very well. For example, when Microsoft made an announcement that it was planning to buy Great Plains, a competitor of salesforce.com, I sent a memo to our staff and forwarded my comments to journalists. Among other things, I explained that "Microsoft Great Plains will cause 'Great Pains' to the software CRM players who built their products in Microsoft's path." Not only was this quote reiterated in many industry articles, some used the "Great Pains" pun in the headline! (Home run.)

I'm a believer in the power of public relations. It's significantly cheaper to encourage a journalist to write a story than it is to buy an ad in the *Wall Street Journal*, where a repeating full-page advertisement in a prime spot can run in excess of a million over the course of a year. That's an unreasonable amount considering that most people won't buy a service because they saw it in an ad. People buy because an expert said it was good or because a user told them about it. Think about it. How many times have you gone to a restaurant based on a giant ad? If you're like me, that has happened very few times. How many times, in contrast, have you followed the recommendation of a friend or a positive review in a magazine or newspaper? Unbiased references by experts carry tremendous power.

Play #25: Make Your Own Metaphors

I spend a lot of time thinking about what I want to say to journalists and *how* I want to say it. I like to come up with simple metaphors to help explain what we are doing and communicate our message. Early on, for example, I said, "salesforce.com is Amazon.com meets Siebel Systems," then it was "AppExchange is the eBay of enterprise software," and later, "Force.com is the Windows Internet operating system."

Metaphors are the simplest way to explain your services and communicate your message. Here's how to do it: relate your product to something that is current and relevant and that everyone understands. Don't forget to test your metaphors before you put them out there. Try a few and run them by customers, analysts, and people in your network to make sure they work. Creating these metaphors takes time up front, but it's well worth it. Journalists on deadline are too pressed for time to come up with their own metaphors, so they use the ones we supply. This further aids our effort to remain consistent and on point with our messaging.

Play #26: No Sacred Cows

Roughly two years after we started our company, George Hu, an analytical and enterprising Stanford MBA student, joined salesforce.com as a summer intern. (Six years later he would lead our global marketing organization.) George was tasked to investigate new vertical markets, such as health care or financial services, for our business to pursue, but on his own initiative he began to examine our sales process and analyze the effectiveness of our marketing dollars. At the time, we were spending $2 to $3 million a month on direct mail and advertising campaigns.

George used the Salesforce application to determine the number of sales leads being generated by our direct mail campaigns. He found that we had fourteen leads in six months. We were shocked, and none of us could believe how much money we were wasting. Although some of the campaigns were extremely successful at differentiating our brand and garnering a firestorm of publicity, George's metrics demonstrated that they weren't winning customers. It was time for a drastic change. After all, it didn't make any sense to create something truly innovative and then rely on tired methods to market and sell it.

This led to a new marketing model, which we based on tactics that were working. (We'll detail those in Part Three.) Keep in mind that the landscape is always changing; you must always examine what's working, evolve your ideas, and change the way you do things.

PART 3

The Events Playbook
How to Use Events to Build Buzz and Drive Business

Play #27: Feed the Word-of-Mouth Phenomenon

As salesforce.com grew, it seemed less necessary to center our marketing on attacking the competition. We evolved our strategy to promote the value of our service. We examined what marketing methods most directly converted into sales and discovered two means that can be used effectively by any company:

- **Editorial**: unbiased business and technology stories in the press
- **Testimony**: the word-of-mouth phenomenon created by customers sharing their success stories with their peers

We reinvented our marketing strategy to harness these two tactics and create forums to allow them to flourish. The idea stemmed from the success we had with our launch party, which proved to us that events were a great way to build buzz and bring in business. We decided to test that idea further with a series of events. The intent was to invite disparate groups—customers, potential users, analysts, press, partners, philanthropists, and nonprofit leaders—and allow them to interact and feed off of one another's energy and insights. Truthfully, we weren't sure whether or not all these constituents would attend, but we decided it was worth a try.

We kicked off our effort with a six-stop "City Tour." In a way, it was similar to a financial road show in which companies introduce themselves to potential investors, but instead of pitching bankers and fund managers, we were meeting with current and prospective customers. The first event was in Philadelphia. We invited fifty people. About fifteen showed up. We did not let that dampen our mood. We acted as if there were four hundred attendees, and we created an incredible enthusiasm around the product. (If you want a successful event, you have to project success; your attitude will help make it a hit.)

Although the first event attracted fewer people than we had hoped, we learned an important lesson: the number of people was less crucial than the mix of people. Excitement stemmed from combining customers and prospects and seating everyone together. This was the antithesis of the way traditional software companies quarantined prospects and journalists from existing customers so that the first group couldn't be poisoned by the second group's negative experiences.

We didn't have to worry about that. Our customers paid month-to-month, so we knew they were happy. It may seem like a gamble to relinquish control and place so much faith in our customers, but the risk paid off. Customers used the open platform they were given to share their enthusiasm about the service. Events proved to be an effective way to maximize the viral effect.

Play #28: Build Street Teams and Leverage Testimony

Although I had been inspired by the customer energy that Steve Jobs had built around the Macintosh, the idea for cultivating a group of salesforce.com enthusiasts did not come from the technology community; it emanated from the hip-hop community. A friend introduced me to MC Hammer, who visited our San Francisco office (wearing a business suit, not the trademark Hammer pants) and shared his "Street Team" concept: that of building local networks of people to back you. At the time, I didn't know how salesforce.com Street Teams would work in action, but I thought that MC Hammer was a creative genius and that this unconventional idea was worth investigating.

Our City Tour program served as a vehicle to extend the salesforce.com message, ignite passion behind the idea, and help us build salesforce.com Street Teams to get customers out and selling for us on a local level.

Each City Tour stop included a keynote address in which I talked about CRM and the pain that had driven the prospects to seek a new alternative. There was also a dedicated time for questions and a live demo of the product. We had assumed that we would field the questions, but instead our customers chimed in with the answers. Initially we were surprised to find ourselves watching from the sidelines as a group of sixty people suddenly

---

Street Teams: Make Customers Part of Your Marketing Force

You've already enlisted employees in the marketing effort by drilling them with key messaging. Now take it to the next level by turning customers into Street Teams:

- Give customers a service or product they love.

- Elicit customers' insight — and use it — so that they'll love what you're offering even more.

- Provide a platform for customers to share their enthusiasm.

- Operate locally to build teams that influence others on a community level and collectively form a global network.

---

broke off into a conversation about how to use our service. However, after seeing this unfold at event after event, we began to recognize what was happening: people weren't attending these events to meet us. They were coming to meet other people using the product.

It was an incredible discovery. We needed to find ways to foster this phenomenon, so we built flexibility into the City Tour program such that there was time for these conversations and exchanges to take place. It was amazing what that allowed: without prompting from us, customers would stand up and deliver spontaneous testimony professing their belief in our product. These users were eager to share their stories.

Around this time, I had the opportunity to meet and speak with the Reverend Billy Graham, and I realized the power of testimony to inspire and influence audiences. I began to think about how to apply an evangelical system to sales. We continued to encourage customers to speak out and share their stories. Rather than address an audience and preach about salesforce.com (prospective customers didn't believe what we said; they believed what customers were experiencing), I began to call on someone from the audience spontaneously and ask her to share her experience.

This morphed into a movement, and our customers soon became salesforce.com evangelists. It made them the best marketing and sales team an organization could have. The unbiased testimonials had an immediate impact on sales. And, over time, this approach earned us a reputation for being open to feedback and being great listeners. We let customers speak their minds and never censored what they said, or tried to quiet trivial concerns when they came up. In fact, we felt that these made the positive comments more believable.

Although we began eliciting these endorsements organically, we soon made customer testimonials a formal part of the City Tour agenda. Prospects frequently had the same questions, and customers were able to address the queries more effectively than we could. We contacted customers in advance of the events and invited them to speak about their experiences. We did not offer payment, yet we found that most users were honored to be invited and eager to participate.

How to Manage—and Succeed with—Customer Testimony

Although every company knows that customer references are important, most companies have a lax approach to managing them, not giving references more focus than a bullet point on a marketing person's to-do list.

References are a fundamental marketing weapon. They are so powerful that we have someone solely dedicated to managing them, and we lead every piece of marketing material with third-party testimony from a customer or analyst.

We also help prepare customers for media interviews or for salesforce.com events like City Tours. (We have three customers speak at every City Tour event in a panel or talk-show-style setting, which allows several customer perspectives and success stories to be told.)

At events, we let anyone speak. I often have an open mic for customers and prospects. Of course it's also essential to have happy and successful customers; otherwise this couldn't work. In a salesforce.com relationship survey (conducted in 2007 and 2008 by independent supplier CustomerStat), 94 percent of customers said they would refer someone, and 74 percent already had—numbers that are twice what most on-premise software vendors are seeing. Leveraging that success has become a key part of our marketing plan.

Play #29: Sell to the End User

Salesforce.com customers are mostly sales, marketing, or customer support people, the people who use traditional enterprise software products. Yet traditional enterprise software companies had never marketed to these people. Enterprise software companies target the executives who control the budget. To us that seemed nonsensical, so we targeted the end users instead and found that they were grateful to finally be given a voice. Our customers—who were brave enough to embrace a product that went against the traditional software establishment—became like a band of savvy rebels, and we celebrated them as such.

We were grateful to these users, and our strategy became centered on nourishing our customer network. We referred to our users as "customer heroes," and blew up giant pictures of them and posted them at events and included them on our materials (with their permission of course). Their companies acknowledged their success too; with salesforce.com, they had achieved a fast implementation and high user adoption, and had made a positive impact on the bottom line. Many, rewarded for these results, rose to new heights in their careers.

Soon we began to see ads on Monster.com and other sites in which employers requested candidates with salesforce.com experience, and resumes in which candidates highlighted "implementing salesforce.com" as a differentiating skill. Later, our customers, such as Matt Evans, formerly a business systems analyst at Tribune Media Services, reported that his new hires expressed excitement about learning the Salesforce application and the ability to put this skill on their resumes in the future. ("That's not the point," Matt replied.) For us, all of this was very telling. By targeting the end user we were creating an economy—with both demand- and supply-side value.

With all this positive energy, our events developed into a salesforce.com love fest. Our customers were proud to share how they used salesforce.com and eager to find out how others did too. Customers were using our terminals or their laptops to log on to the salesforce.com Web site and look at one another's applications.

As our customers were evangelizing about our product, they were having a good time as well. We began to notice that there were salesforce.com groupies who came to an event every time we were in town. They always left with a stack of business cards, and many of them kept in touch. Each City Tour event cost about $250 per attendee—significantly less than the traditional advertising we had been doing and much more effective. When a prospect came to one of our events, about 80 percent of the time we were able to close the deal. Appealing directly to the people who used the service made all the difference.

Play #30: The Event *Is* the Message

It would be remiss not to mention that we made a few errors with the first of our City Tours. Many ran too long. One was held in the dingy basement of a budget hotel, which was a mistake. Selecting the right site is important—the location should be one that reflects what you want to say about your brand. If you are selling a high-quality service, your events must offer a high-quality experience. We now host events at four- or five-star hotels or world-class restaurants and try to book the newest, most exciting, or highest-rated venues in town to attract attendees. These are the values we want to have people associate with us.

You must always view an event as an opportunity to reflect—and extend—your image. For example, we extend our promotion of on-demand technologies to include self-service kiosks (similar to those in the airports) to allow attendees to quickly and easily check in to our events. Let the personality of your company shine, and that means be consistent. If you are about innovation, make sure your event embraces the spirit of innovation. If you are about sustainability and responsibility, make sure the chocolate you give out as a favor is fair-trade!

The Host's Playbook: How to Throw a Great Event

- Many companies mistakenly think they just have to hold an event. Wrong. If you're going to do it, do it right.

- If you want a successful event, you have to act like it's a success; your attitude becomes a self-fulfilling prophesy.

- The number of people is far less crucial than the mix of people: seat prospects, journalists, and customers together.

- Harness your customers' positive energy and make them part of your marketing force. People will talk about you whether you like it or not — why not provide the forum?

- The event is the message. Ensure that every decision you make — from venue to food to speakers — reflects well on your business and conveys your message.

- A top-tier venue can attract attendees and make your business look established.

- Make sure your quality service is reflected in every aspect of the event, from the invitations you design to the confirmation e-mail you send — even to such details as having name badges ready with names spelled correctly.

- Have enough people manning the doors to prevent a long wait to get in. Your guests should feel your warm welcome from the moment they arrive.

- Every employee at the event must be on message and look the part. Prep team members to handle different scenarios and recognize your attendees. Remember: one individual can ruin the whole event by brushing someone off or giving an answer that is not accurate.

- Networking is a vital part of every event. Help attendees meet each other, exchange contact information, join your community, and learn from one another. We host a networking reception to wrap up every event; it's a great way to get attendees to talk to each other, meet our partners, and quiz our product experts. These networking events usually happen inside the exhibition area to leverage the energy of the live demos.

- Make your event fun as well as informative. We've had great results inviting visionaries, such as Colin Powell, Neil Young, and Malcolm Gladwell, to speak at our events.

- Your event must look effortless. Spend the necessary time to plan and make sure that all your technology and demonstrations work flawlessly — do a practice run.

- Capture customer testimonials onsite at the event. We have photographers and videographers to photograph and record our most successful customers sharing their stories about how our service has changed their business. (We follow up after the event to get their approval to use these great new customer testimonials across all of our marketing properties.)

- Provide every attendee with the most relevant next steps to become even more successful. For example, the next step might be a free trial of a new product, or it could be a special offer on training. Ask yourself, "What do I want the attendee to do next?" and then craft the post-event experience that will allow him or her to take action.

- Put content from your event on your Web site, your company's Facebook page, and YouTube to allow your message to continue to circulate long after the event is over.

Play #31: Reduce Costs and Increase Impact

We fine-tuned our events strategy so that each event was hosted at a great venue, and we developed a formula that included a keynote address, a presentation from at least one or two customers who fielded questions, a demo, and a cocktail party. Yes, you read that last one right.

The inspiration for the happy hour started in New York City. We were doing our usual dog-and-pony show at a hotel near Wall Street. After the presentation, more than half the audience lingered, and after about thirty minutes, the cleaning crew came in and kicked everyone out. Not wanting to lose the momentum of this exciting exchange, I invited everyone down to the hotel bar. Almost everyone accepted. Two hours later, after the group had cleared out, I reflected on the unbelievable scenario that had just unfolded. Several prospects had been converted into customers while I did little more than sit back and have an iced tea.

We knew that the secret to creating successful events was bringing customers and prospects together. The Wall Street after-hours customer Q&A demonstrated that we could maximize the positive effects by offering everyone additional opportunities to mix informally. From that experience on, we budgeted for a cocktail mixer at the end of every City Tour presentation.

We also discovered that attendees loved to boot up their laptops and play around on the application and investigate new features. That encouraged us to add an "Expo" with our booths and the booths of our business partners (who built applications that worked with Salesforce or helped implement our service) as a way for attendees to learn about everything that was available.

Our partners were aware of the traffic our events drew, so they were eager to participate. In fact, they were even willing to share the hosting costs.

Everyone loved the City Tours, but as they became more popular, we found that we couldn't afford to run them in every city. We came up with a solution when an East Coast salesman said, "I don't need or even want the content. I just want to have the social mixer—high-end drinks and appetizers with customers."

It was unconventional, but we like unconventional, so we decided it was worth a try. We planned a small cocktail party at the Grand Havana Room in New York. Eleven customers and prospects came, and there were eight people from our company. We drank scotch and smoked cigars and talked about salesforce.com. The bill was almost one-tenth of a standard City Tour, but the net effect was virtually the same. Customers learned from one other, and the prospects were swept up by the customers' gusto.

When marketing executive Phill Robinson joined us to build the European market, he told me he didn't understand the point of these so-called Club Events. "You get customers and prospects together, but you have no business content and no demonstration," he said incredulously. Phill's dubiousness was not surprising, considering he had been with our competitor for seven years and was not yet reformed. "Why would you get them together if you're not going to pitch them? What do you do?"

What we do is quite simple. We rely on the quality of the product and provide an opportunity for the product to be discussed. The most effective selling is done not by a sales team but by people you don't even know who are talking about your products without your being aware of it. In this era, those conversations are more frequent and more public than ever. They are not happening behind closed doors, but 24/7 in the blogosphere and on social networking sites. Instead of fearing

Get Your Game Plan Ready

There's a lot of prep work necessary to execute a flawless event.

- Develop your plan to acquire contacts. Define success metrics. Set your lead goal and determine your target conversion and close rates.

- Establish a follow-up process before the event. Develop all communication materials, e-mails, and call scripts. Execute the plan within a few days of the event.

- Create an exciting giveaway to draw traffic to your event (or booth at your trade show). Consider hot products — for example, we've seen success with iPhones, MacBooks, and Nintendo Wiis.

- Have a compelling offer, such as an exclusive discount on your product or service, for target attendees.

- Provide content that validates your ideas. White papers or best practices documentation by third parties is effective.

- Leverage complementary partnerships. Invite business partners to collaborate with you in planning and hosting an event, or team up with complementary partners at trade shows to drive traffic to one another's area.

- Create a takeaway piece for attendees that includes your offer, contact information, and quotes from successful customers and other third-party validation.

these public conversations, companies must cater to them and leverage them. By providing a forum for customers to meet, you can be a participant in these exchanges and use the viral effect to your advantage.

Play #32: Always Stay in the Forefront

In order to remain relevant, you must establish yourself as a thought leader in your industry. Be the canary in the coal mine, warning people of what's ahead—and demonstrate how your company is shaping the future. Events are an effective way to deliver your message to your audience and the press (which then reiterates it to a wider audience).

We hold "launch events" every six to eight weeks. That's the period of time within which I believe something new should be introduced to the press. I deliver the keynote, in which we always announce some news (an acquisition, a partnership, or a product) as well as talk about the future direction of the industry and our role in it. These events, held in such top press markets as New York, San Francisco, and London, give us an opportunity to stay in the forefront and remain relevant. These events are the drumbeat of our marketing strategy: the volume of media coverage always increases on the heels of a launch event. The number of people visiting the Web site increases, and the number of leads increases. Most important, revenue increases.

Play #33: The Truth About Competition (It *Is* Good for Everyone)

Although our events have been spectacularly effective at drawing traffic, one incident created the biggest percentage gain in traffic to the salesforce.com site (up until that time). We didn't plan this one, but we may have played a role in causing it. In October 2003, after years of denouncing the SaaS model that we had been trailblazing, Siebel Systems announced that it would launch a Siebel CRM on-demand service. Less than two weeks later, it bought UpShot, a provider of on-demand enterprise software.

Our biggest competitor had finally seen the power of the Internet as the next platform. Whereas the giant's step into our territory might have threatened some young companies, we knew this was exactly what we needed. After all, it was our goal to create an industry, not just a company. Siebel's entry into the space endorsed our model. Our competitor became our karmic partner.

With Siebel's news, we'd finally succeeded at initiating a *market*. A market doesn't exist until there is a competitor, and ideally two or three competitors. Competition is good. In the case of Siebel-UpShot, it was very good. The announcement of its on-demand play almost doubled our business virtually overnight because it validated our model. Don't fear competition: welcome it and leverage it.

Play #34: Be Prepared for Every Scenario ... and Have Fun

After a few years, our City Tours became so deluged with attendees that there was standing room only. The next step was an annual user conference where we would have the opportunity to fuel camaraderie and further strengthen our community of evangelists. We named this event Dreamforce. Unlike a City Tour event, which ran for a few hours, the annual Dreamforce event was held over the course of a few days. Our first Dreamforce attracted more than a thousand attendees from countries as far away as Australia, Cameroon, and Israel, but it was our second Dreamforce that taught us some of our most valuable lessons in event planning.

Dreamforce 2004 was slated for the beginning of November—kicking off on the day of the U.S. presidential election. It wasn't an ideal time to hold a conference that had people traveling from all over the country, but we had a good reason. It was the Hilton San Francisco's only available time.

The problem of election timing paled in comparison to what happened next. Two weeks before the conference, all San Francisco hotel employees went on strike. Apprehensive that we would be without a venue to host our biggest event of the year, we planned for two scenarios: Plan A, in which the hotel workers ended the strike in time to host our conference, and Plan B, in which the hotel workers stayed on strike. We had two versions of everything, including conference guides and staffing crews. It turned out that the strike continued, so it was fortunate we had planned for a comprehensive Plan B. Sure enough, Plan B turned out to be better. We kept part of the conference at the Hilton and moved many of the presentations to off-site locations that could accommodate us without our having to cross the hotel picket lines. We planned for the keynote to be held in the Golden Gate Theater, a few blocks from the Hilton, which allowed us to stretch our creative wings in a professional theater space.

Almost three thousand people showed up (more than twice the number we'd had the previous year), and while attendees were anticipating presentations from industry leaders, we also gave them an election-day surprise. After I introduced myself and began to deliver my address, marketing executive Clarence

So walked onto the stage, whispered to me, and handed me a piece of paper.

"I have just been informed that the president is here," I said. "He told me he might swing by, but I didn't believe it."

The presidential music began to play, the eagle insignia flashed on the screens, and "President" George W. Bush walked onto the stage. Actually, it was a really good fake president, the terrific impersonator Steve Bridges, whom we hired to kick off Dreamforce 2004 with an Election Day comedy sketch.

When the "president" finished the routine, I went back on stage and delivered the keynote. We've always loved doing fun things like that—and turning what others may have seen as a hardship into an opportunity to create something great.

Play #35: Seize Unlikely Opportunities to Stay Relevant

Some people believe in luck or karma. They certainly exist, but only for those who have the mind-set to see them. It was the opening morning of Dreamforce in 2005, the biggest day of the year for salesforce.com, and my fiancée was suffering with sympathy anxiety prior to my keynote address and couldn't sleep. Scouring the Internet at 4:30 A.M., she discovered that Oracle had made an early morning announcement: Oracle had agreed to buy Siebel. This was uncanny timing.

She woke me knowing that I would have to move quickly to acknowledge this colossal news. I thought this was the gift of the century and jumped to take advantage of it. The marketing team was at my house immediately, and we secured an interview on CNBC, where I was able to comment on Oracle's lack of innovation and predict Siebel's death. We completely reworked the entire keynote address that had been planned for months to focus on this landmark event and to illustrate how the on-demand model had become powerful enough to kill our enormous competitor. We played the CNBC news broadcast on TV screens around Moscone Center West. The timing was so auspicious and the broadcast was viewed as such a coup that many people thought the whole thing was staged!

This was a victory for salesforce.com and the on-demand industry we had helped spawn. It was evident that we were accelerating to the next level. Consolidation in the client-server computing industry was opening the door for SaaS. Reporters came to Dreamforce simply to see what I would say about the news. They not only published stories that included our insight but also mentioned that it was our annual user week. We were mentioned in nearly every Siebel-Oracle story, and our event got more press than even I could have anticipated.

The industry was going gangbusters dissecting the Siebel acquisition, and the general opinion was in keeping with mine that the opportunity to be the global leader in the CRM market had opened for salesforce.com. (One outlet even ran the internal memo I sent to our staff and printed, "Benioff is right."[1] It also said that Siebel was a "dinosaur" that was now extinct and that "consolidation of the old guard of enterprise software will continue as software purchasing continues to shift to On Demand vendors.") Even Bruce Cleveland, formerly Siebel's senior vice president and general manager of on-demand, later reflected, "If you read what was in the press, you would think salesforce.com was eating Siebel's lunch." We had worked tirelessly for many years to lay the groundwork for this.

Play #36: Stay Scrappy . . . but Not Too Scrappy

We knew that we had truly emerged as the unrivaled market leader in the eyes of the industry when we arrived at Dreamforce 2006 to find that a handful of employees from a small CRM company had set up a mock protest outside the convention center. I'm not really sure what they were protesting, and it was a small, low-budget, and poorly executed rip-off of the types of tactics we had invented, but that wasn't the point. The point was that we knew not to get ruffled.

We did not want this company to get free PR on our coattails! Ignoring this escapade worked well. A blogger asked a Dreamforce attendee if she had seen what was going on outside when she arrived, and she replied that it must have been some kind of salesforce.com stunt. (Note: if you are going to compete with someone at his or her own game, always remember to step up the innovation.)

Most of all, our smaller competitor's stunt didn't work because we never forgot or underestimated the lessons we've learned. We've seen what happens when bigger companies act defensively and validate small competitors. No one should ever make that mistake.

We might be the market leader now, but that doesn't mean we're complacent or see our work as done. We have evolved our mission from replacing one legacy company to toppling the entire traditional software establishment to transforming the entire industry. Our current battle: we have to save the customer from Microsoft, Oracle, and SAP.

Our current strategy: evolving our unconventional tactics to beat bigger competitors and overcome new challenges. When Microsoft announced a platform to allow developers to create applications that can be accessed via the Internet (an idea that eerily echoed our own offering), we were ready to respond. Members of our team descended on Microsoft's launch event. They circled the Los Angeles Convention Center on bicycles and handed out salesforce.com T-shirts, doughnuts, and fliers pitching our Force.com platform as "the fastest and easiest way to build, buy and run business applications." In an effort to sway Microsoft's crowd of developers to sign up for our service (and further needle our opponent), we gave away five new computers. Of course they weren't PCs. They were MacBook Air notebooks!

We may be a big company now, but we'll never forget where we came from or the core values and spirited efforts that got us where we are today. Furthermore, we've never abandoned the importance of having fun.

Underdog to Market Leader

Strategies evolve as your role shifts, but you should continue to

- Plan killer events.
- Continue big-bang efforts with the press.
- Heavily invest in customers' success and leverage their voice (use customers to sell new products, reach into new accounts, and speak to the press).

PART 4

The Sales Playbook
How to Energize Your Customers into a Million-Member Sales Team

Play #37: Give It Away

In typical salesforce.com style, our initial sales strategy went completely against convention. In a response that was becoming just as predictable, countless people told us that it would never work.

Historically, enterprise software companies sold their products for vast amounts of money according to a very defined system. Their process involved sending out white papers, visiting prospects in their offices, and delivering a highly customized demonstration. After months of work and several rounds of negotiations, the company closed a multilicense deal. The vendor collected the bill up front, leaving the customer carrying the entire risk.

That process didn't make any sense to us. All the old-school laborious and high-cost selling steps were no longer necessary. We had entered the new era of the Internet, and our service was available 24/7 on the Web. It was so simple that customers could learn everything about it, subscribe, and get it running just by visiting www.salesforce.com. It was do-it-yourself. There were no analysts and no meetings. Further, there was no haggling. The service cost $50 per user per month for everyone, and customers paid as they went.

Upending that part of the enterprise software selling status quo was enough to warrant some quizzical comments, but one strategy in particular sealed our skeptics' doubt: we gave our service away for free in the beginning. This was a key part of our seed-and-grow strategy, which assumed that if we planted a seed in the ground and nurtured it appropriately, we would soon see the fruits of our labors. In order to prep that proverbial ground, we offered a free functional trial for five users for a year. The trial was open to anyone who expressed interest in salesforce.com; this individual didn't even have to speak with a salesperson.

Although a free trial has evolved into the industry standard, this was not the case in 1999. No software company allowed a prospect to use the entire service at no cost. We recognized that prospects wanted to feel assured that we were accurately representing our service's capabilities, so we needed to let them experience it for themselves. Admittedly, the plan was self-serving. Offering the service for free increased our opportunities to gain valuable feedback, which we knew was the secret to creating a successful product.

Play #38: Win First Customers by Treating Them Like Partners

Thanks to our developers' talent and our earliest test users' (read: friends' and former colleagues') guidance, we developed a quality beta application. Finally, it was time to go out and win actual customers. Suddenly, we stumbled upon our newest and biggest test: making people comfortable putting their most sensitive data (proprietary customer lists) on our servers. Everyone was concerned about security breaches. It was challenging to convince prospects to try our service, and it was especially challenging to convince the first one. Most people don't want to be the first to take a giant risk. Realizing that truism was pivotal. We finessed our strategy to target pioneers who saw an opportunity to participate in something new and exciting.

That first pioneer came in the form of Blue Martini Software, one of the small software companies in which I had previously invested. I knew I was asking for a favor when I called the founder, Monte Zweben, but I also knew I was offering something that he really needed. Monte's sales team was using spreadsheets and wanted a CRM system, but it couldn't afford traditional enterprise software. Blue Martini also needed a service without the complexities of enterprise software, because Monte wanted his sales team to be focused on selling, not getting a system up and running.

Monte floated the idea of using our new service by his sales force (the end users), and they immediately embraced it. Blue Martini (which has since been acquired and is now known as Escalate Retail) became our first customer in August 1999. The service was up and running within two weeks—not the months or years by which other software implementations were measured. Even better, Blue Martini did not have to make a million-dollar investment.

We did not have a formal sales organization at this time so in our quest for early customers, everyone on the salesforce.com team was encouraged to contact anyone he or she knew in any industry, or at any start-up. Diane Mark, our product manager, won our second client while she was standing in line at the local market, Mollie Stone's. She ran into a former colleague who was working as a sales manager at iSyndicate, a company that sold syndicated content over the Web. She asked him what the company used to manage its sales process.

"ACT! and Excel," he replied. "It's a mess." After a short meeting with the iSyndicate executives, they signed on as our second customer. By September, we had five pilot customers using salesforce.com for free. They were more like beta customers, but I called them design partners to recognize their real contributions.

Our design partners' insights were essential to the development of our application. We contacted them frequently to discuss their experience using the service, and they became the eyes and ears of the engineering team. They discovered features and tools and functionalities that they needed. We added a button that allowed any user to immediately send us an idea, and we could react very quickly. We created "bugforce," a scaled-down database to track bugs and new ideas, which helped us rate the frequency of the problems or requests. The development team built all additional functionality in a very short time—a matter of weeks, which was unheard of in the industry. Being small, nimble, and in constant communication with our earliest customers is what enabled us to produce a terrific service.

In fall 1999, once we had honed the service into something of measurable value to customers, we hired our first dedicated salesperson (and fifteenth employee) to help acquire additional free users and to convert our free users into paying customers. The plan worked exactly as intended. Blue Martini soon started paying for the service. Before long, Colo.com, a datacenter provider, was paying for twenty-five sales reps to use salesforce.com and touting our service in the press, explaining that it cost a fraction of a traditional enterprise product.

Our conversion strategy was successful for several reasons. First, through the free trial, prospects had already experienced the service, and they knew it worked. Second, it was a very low risk proposition because the service was billed monthly and there was freedom to change the plan or quit without any penalties. Third, it was such a good product that users became addicted. They needed it.

Go from Adoption to Addiction with a Feedback Loop

Be open to including all customers, and treat them as *partners*. To do so, utilize a fast and prioritized "feedback loop":

1. Stay in touch with customers.

2. Develop a way to track their requests.

3. Respond to their requests quickly.

4. Ask if their needs have been satisfactorily met.

5. Pay attention to how they are using the product.

Play #39: Let Your Web Site Be a Sales Rep

We were growing with our existing customers, and our nascent sales team was landing new customers, and then something extraordinary happened that accelerated everything. In December 1999, an article titled "Salesforce.com Takes the Lead in Latest Software Revolution" appeared in the *Wall Street Journal*.

The story was written by Don Clark, a journalist I had invited to the Laboratory to meet the developers and test the product while we were still developing the prototype. My cofounders had been angry with me for speaking with a journalist so early in our development process, but it turned out to have been worth the risk (and their wrath). This was the second time that Don Clark wrote about us. Whereas Clark's previous story had mentioned salesforce.com as part of the exciting trend of software moving online, this one, which appeared only eight months after we were founded (and two months before we officially launched) focused entirely on us.

The day after the article came out, the phones began ringing like mad. We were inundated with leads. More than a hundred people came to our Web site and requested information.

We didn't even have a sales process developed to deal with the level of interest. (We had a Web site, but we didn't have any people to follow through.) Peter Wooster, the first salesperson, was still the only member of the sales "team," and he was buried in qualified leads, implementing programs over the weekend and training customers on how to use the service during the beginning of the week.

The *Journal* article encouraged users from companies of all sizes to register for the free trial—even salespeople at such megacorporations as Xerox and Siemens. This strategy also created a unique sales phenomenon: before most prospective customers heard from somebody at salesforce.com, they were already using the service.

Before you have a single sales rep, you can invest in your Web site and let it do some selling. A good Web site is more effective than any direct marketing campaign. A lead capture screen, where visitors are required to enter their contact information, is an effective way to find hot leads. It's essential to keep a Web site easy to use and fresh with regular updates.

Play #40: Make Every Customer a Member of Your Sales Team

Just as we tapped every employee as a marketing person, we believed that every customer could serve as a salesperson. Inside every customer there was unrealized potential. By offering training and support, we could build a sales army that was not limited to a finite number of salesforce.com salespeople, but could scale to hundreds of thousands—and, one day, millions—of customer salespeople.

The sales and marketing teams must work together to foster evangelists and build a sales army. At any company, the marketing department and sales department must be best friends. It's necessary to play together, partner together, and ultimately succeed together.

Although I believed that a service that was easy to purchase, easy to learn, and easy to use would sell itself, I also understood that we needed to build a process for selling and a strong sales team to capture and qualify leads and to close deals.

At the time that we reinvented our marketing strategy to be focused on leveraging editorial opportunities and customer testimony, we created a formal "process" around marketing and sales. We came up with the diagram shown in Figure 4.1.

The heart of marketing was our internal database of leads—the core that kept our company ticking. Early on, the free trials were one of the best methods of capturing leads (we were able to collect names and contact information easily in exchange for the free trial), and we needed to investigate what other methods we could systematically employ to drive additional leads. We evaluated sources of leads—word of mouth, Internet search, press activity, and direct marketing e-mails—and listed them on the left-hand side of our heart. Next, we cemented our follow-up strategy by creating a system to track the action the prospect had taken (contacted us, registered for an event), and we committed to follow up on any lead within twenty-four hours, whether the lead came from the CIO of a Fortune 500 company or a university student. After all, this was the beginning of a relationship, and we wanted to provide a very positive customer experience from the start.

We devised a plan for the marketing team to work with the sales representatives and provide scripts, templates, and training so that everyone would have the correct positioning and latest offers. The sales team classified the leads into categories (working leads, qualified leads) and aimed to push them through to a deal using myriad delivery tools and content that we created for various stages in the lead cycle.

The goal was to convert a lead to a deal in thirty to ninety days. If the deal didn't close, it wasn't tossed, but was kept active

Figure 4.1. 90-Day Campaigns to Cash to Customer Cycle

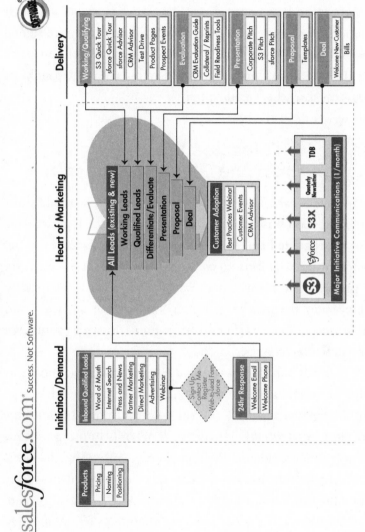

in an archive of warm leads. We found that by continuing to cultivate the relationship, we were likely to make the sale eventually.

The cycle doesn't end with a signed deal. Because we use a subscription-based model, we have to invest just as much effort in making our customers successful once they are signed on—otherwise they'll leave. We created a system of best practices (including customer events and webinars) to help support customers and keep them happy.

Play #41: Telesales Works (Even Though Everyone Thinks It Doesn't)

If this was a war against the software industry model, our marketing team was our Air Force, providing the high-level air cover necessary to blanket the zone with our message. It was the mission of the sales force to conduct the one-on-one combat on the ground. The truth is that many of the techniques initially employed by the sales team weren't innovative, but we found that investing time and demonstrating tenacity were simple and effective selling strategies.

This was still the era of the dot-com brouhaha, and I was invited to several parties every night. I would speak with a large number of people and collect business cards from everyone. The next morning, I would give the stack of cards to the sales team and urge them to contact the leads immediately. They hated it. They tried to hide as they saw me walk down the hallway, but luckily the office was a big open space, and there was nowhere for them to go. I also encouraged the team to call everyone they knew and to routinely ask friends of friends for referrals. Those friends sometimes got aggravated, but we got users. They were my favorite kind of users because the leads were free!

When salesforce.com was founded, there was a preconceived notion that you could not sell CRM applications over the phone. Companies were investing massive amounts in building high-touch teams that operated in far-flung offices. We broke that mold—mostly because we couldn't afford to follow it in the traditional way—and proved that telesales could win a high close rate at one-third the cost and in one-third the amount of the time as the traditional selling model.

Although our approach is similar to what other companies might call telesales, we called it our "corporate sales" model and found that recruits responded more positively to that term. We built the corporate sales team with recent graduates from great colleges who were terrific at answering the incoming calls. These individuals were smart and energetic, and were closing sales without much training. We also built a team of more experienced "outbound sales" reps who were calling out and closing deals. We offered an extensive training boot camp and gave sales reps three to six months to build a pipeline. (They were then expected to close business, and those who didn't perform were moved elsewhere.)

Customers were curious about the lack of a face-to-face meeting at first, but soon they appreciated the calls and Web demos as effective time-savers for everyone. This practice would become more relevant later, when the economy faltered and all corporations slashed their travel budgets and began communicating via Web conferencing and conference calls. Although we did not predict the shift, our strategy, born of necessary frugality, prepared us to take advantage of it. As technology advances with better Web conferencing tools and new and less expensive ways to connect people more easily, this is the best way for any company to get its sales team up and running.

Outline for a Sales Call: The Top Five Points for a
Winning Conversation

1. Leverage the experience the prospect has had with other solutions.
2. Introduce the value your product offers.
3. Provide success stories from customers. (Build and maintain a strong referral program.)
4. Verify success stories by offering customer testimony.
5. Provide a customer for the prospect to contact.

Play #42: Don't Dis Your First Product with a Discount

Many of our sales reps who came from the enterprise software industry were accustomed to offering a discount. The discount had become their closing strategy when they had to make their targets. I didn't think we needed that motivator, and I believed that our service was fairly priced. Discounts, I thought, were tied to perceived risk. Offering deals would compromise the service's value.

Most important, by keeping the price the same for everyone, we kept the costs low for everyone. It was the most democratic way. Unlike the rest of the industry, we charged the same per seat, whether someone wanted two licenses or two hundred. Why should someone pay less just because his or her company was bigger? That didn't seem fair. I was unyielding on this. I heard the jokes behind my back that I wouldn't give even my grandmother a discount. It's true; I couldn't—that would ruin the democratic model on which salesforce.com was built. (She paid full price.)

Unable to rely on a discount to close a deal, our salespeople actually became even better. Instead of waiting to push extra hard at the end of the quarter, they pushed to close deals immediately all year. The urgency to sell became about the customer's need for our service, not about the salesperson's need to make a quarterly quota. Our selling strategy—to be priced to the value of the market, keep costs low, and not favor anyone—not only was effective at closing deals but also became an essential part of our brand.

Once a company is more established, there are reasons to implement different price structures, but don't get your product off to the wrong start by undervaluing it.

Play #43: Sales Is a Numbers Game

In an effort to be totally customer focused, we made it our policy to immediately respond to any lead regardless of its size. There was so much activity that before long our salespeople were closing $50,000 to $70,000 per salesperson per month. We quickly discovered that the more salespeople we hired, the more we saw revenue increase. This proved that we couldn't simply encourage salespeople to sell more. We needed to increase the number of salespeople. This was the key to growing revenue.

Nine times out of ten, companies fail because they don't set up a large enough sales force and thus have no way to collect enough revenue. Don't skimp on sales reps: 25 to 50 percent of the employee base should be salespeople who report to the head of sales. (Half of our company is in sales.)

When you are in a growth phase, use cash to hire—and hire, hire, hire! You have to grow the distribution capacity by having as many salespeople as you can and by organizing and managing the sales team to ensure productivity. At the same time, it's necessary to motivate individuals to close as much business as possible. There is a huge difference between a $50,000 month and a $60,000 month multiplied by every salesperson over time.

Play #44: Segment the Markets

We launched salesforce.com as a democratizing service, without dedicating resources to target markets of specific size. In particular, we were concerned about investing too much in the small business market, an audience that made sense for us, but one where the cost of collecting was likely to be exorbitantly high compared to the revenue generated. In addition, there was worry about potential attrition. (Only about two-thirds of new employer firms survive at least two years, and about 44 percent survive at least four, according to the U.S. Small Business Association.)

Rob Acker, a former Oracle sales manager who joined us in spring 2000 to build a lead generation team and an account management team, encouraged us to refine our strategy and target particular audiences. His suggestion was spurred by his observations. Rob was responsible for tracking incoming leads and how many seats were eventually purchased. He knew every single detail about every customer. He had to—in a quest to learn what was working, I'd often ask specific questions: "How's the *BusinessWeek* ad doing? How many calls did you get? How many leads do you have?"

After tracking every metric, Rob noticed the success we were experiencing with small companies (businesses with fewer than thirty employees). He approached me with the idea to ramp up our efforts to specifically target the very small business market, which he found to be progressive in its support of new technology: "There's a huge opportunity," he said. "We're thinking this isn't profitable, but this might be a gold mine. Just give me one guy."

I had been focused on building other areas of the business, and because we were still a small company, we had to be very careful about outlaying too many resources. I also wanted to see how seriously Rob had considered his plan. (I often vet ideas by playing the devil's advocate or arguing to see if someone will defend them.) I mentioned my concerns to Rob, and he responded with conviction that he believed this was the right idea. He had research to support his claim that small business was going to be extremely profitable. Rob was passionate about taking advantage of this opportunity, and I trusted that he could make it work. "Take four people," I told him.

It turned out to be a very good decision to focus more attention on smaller businesses. The close rates were higher, and the sales time and cost of sale were low. We experienced phenomenal growth in this area and expanded from four sales reps to twenty reps in just six months.

Segmenting the markets made sense, and I was reminded of the value of listening to our people. Employees are deeply invested in the organization where they work, and they often have worthy ideas about how to make it a better place. Tell them that you'd like to hear from them—and make time to listen.

Play #45: Leverage Times of Change

Because of our mandate to target small business, and in what was probably a reflection of the times, a large proportion of our customers in the early days were Internet start-ups. They shared our appreciation of the Internet, they were early adopters of technology, and they were growing at a wild pace. It seemed that our dot-com customers were calling every day to add new subscriptions. Online search site LookSmart went from five subscriptions to fifty in one month. Our business was booming, and it was largely fueled by the dot-com fury.

Then, suddenly, everything started to unravel. Many dot-coms, once flush with venture capital money, began to run out of cash. As many of these companies struggled to survive, we had to deal with the ugly consequences of very serious user attrition. Whereas some of our customers reduced the number of users, others pulled out entirely and then folded. By October 2001, the crash had deeply affected our business. We were burning through $1 million to $1.5 million every month, and we were severely cash flow negative. The potential for bankruptcy was at hand.

We needed to implement a new strategy to improve cash flow, and we found ourselves in a seemingly disastrous predicament. Investors were spooked, and valuations were appallingly low, making it an awful time to raise capital. Furthermore, I wouldn't have wanted to raise money even had this been the best of fundraising times—additional financing would have diluted the value of all of the original investors' shares.

On the heels of several unfruitful meetings with venture capitalists (see Part Eight for those horror stories), Magdalena Yesil, our first investor and a very active member of our board, approached me with an idea. She believed that our monthly billing plan, which was meant to be a low-risk proposition for customers, was jeopardizing the financial security of our company. Magdalena suggested that we change our strategy to collecting for a year or more up front and offering a discount as an incentive. Her analysis demonstrated that this would solve our cash flow problem, which was largely created by paying our sales reps a commission based on a twelve-month deal, while only collecting revenue from our customers one month at a time. It was taking two to three months to recoup our expenses on each deal—and that was in the best of circumstances.

This was hardly the best of circumstances, though. We were in the midst of the dot-com meltdown and were losing accounts. We realized that many of the accounts we had lost had been with us for less than a year, meaning that we never recouped our expenses. Further, managing billing around a month-to-month customer was, by itself, costing us a fortune. Carl Schachter and Brian Millham, members of our team who focused on business development and sales, had, like Magdalena, come to believe that we needed to change the way we structured deals. They investigated what other companies were doing to capture commitment and spent a day with a partner of ours to gain an understanding of how it was securing commitments by selling contracts. Carl and Brian took everything they learned back to salesforce.com and began to consider how it could be adapted to our business.

Although this idea to sell annual or multiannual contracts and to encourage the commitment with a discount may seem like a simple one and may even seem obvious in hindsight, it represented a dramatic shift for our company. Our team was divided as to what we should do; several of us wanted to maintain our no-contract and no-discount policy. After all, we had publicly touted these differentiators. Could we suddenly change? Would customers be willing to make this switch?

Ultimately, we needed to make this change in order to survive. We created two factors to justify a discount: the total number of users and the length of the contract. We offered existing customers the opportunity to continue with the price of $50 per person per month if they signed an annual contract and paid us cash up front. (We still recognized the revenue monthly, but this approach would cement the customer's commitment, help with billing and collections costs, and improve our cash position.) If customers preferred to continue month-to-month, the rate would be our new price of $65 a month. Although we thought the plan was fair and attractive, it was nevertheless a great shock to us when about half our customers immediately agreed to it.

Our customers were willing to accept the change because we had earned their trust and their loyalty. Our customers, it turns out, were rooting for us to succeed. We were also established enough by this point that about 20 percent of our new customers accepted the plan right away. Many of these customers said that they were motivated by the price discount, and they believed that paying on an annual basis was simpler than dealing with a monthly billing cycle. Whereas I had always been concerned that customers would feel constricted by an annual contract, it turned out that many of them saw it as a good opportunity to lock in favorable terms.

Of course—as we had suspected—there was a fair share of customers who were not pleased with the change. I would even go as far as to describe a handful of them as outraged. Concerned that we could lose these customers and wanting to provide a solution that would quell their anger, we offered to grandfather them in with the old price and month-to-month payment schedule for one year. It was challenging to maintain, but it kept them satisfied, and eventually earned their long-term business.

In an effort to ensure execution of our new plan, we wanted to create an incentive to spur sales reps to close annual deals. "Let's give sales reps 50 percent higher commissions to sign annual deals," said Frank van Veenendaal, who had joined us to help build the sales team (and had always hated the no-contract premise). Frank recommended that we pay the reps two months' worth of sales revenue for every twelve-month contract. Under this innovative new arrangement, sales reps would be motivated by the financial rewards of capturing a longer commitment, and we would still keep ten months of revenue in the bank.

That decision had a significant ramification on our growth. By collecting up front—and offering sales reps a real motivator to ensure that we closed multiyear deals—we went from cash flow negative to cash flow positive in less than a year. We made this new structure part of our official compensation plan—and it's largely why we've been able to continue to grow an impressive amount of cash on the balance sheet to this day.

Listening Is an Underrated Virtue

There is only one way to get customer support: earn it. If you deliver on your promises and treat customers well, you will earn their trust and loyalty. That makes customers root for your company and its success.

Through open communication and transparency you can keep customer trust, and even make changes they may dislike without losing them. Do not make changes without their permission or without giving them a choice. (Coca-Cola learned this the hard way when customers revolted against "the new taste of Coca-Cola." They hadn't asked for this sweeter formulation, they didn't want a new Coke, and they didn't buy it. Only by listening to customers and then reintroducing the original Coke did the company regain loyalty and sales.)

Customers need to be aware of changes that are happening — and they need to feel as if their needs are considered in the company's decisions.

Play #46: Your Seeds Are Sown, so Grow, Grow, Grow

Like all new companies, salesforce.com was focused on survival in its earliest years. We had to educate the masses about the SaaS model and demonstrate that it worked. Once we finally proved that, we needed to devise a strategy to take our company to the next level. We needed to improve cash flow—and we needed to grow, and grow *fast*.

In the very beginning, we cast a big net, fishing for any customer who bit. For the most part, we caught a lot of minnows, and then, as we became more established, we attracted some tuna. Many of our minnows got washed away in the dot-com crash, but the bigger fish, such as American Medical Response and Analog Devices, found our elastic service fitting for precarious times, and they weathered the storm with us. We realized that it was time to target further upstream. With the product's success well established, winning enterprise business became a formal objective.

It was clear that this endeavor would require massive organizational changes. Creating a world-class field sales force—the kind of team we needed to win large deals—was not an easy proposition. As much as we had wished to win enterprise companies in the past, and even made some lackluster efforts to do so, we did not have the distribution or distribution capacity in place to make this a sustainable pursuit.

Building distribution is a tremendous challenge: it's expensive, it's time-consuming, and it's always evolving (especially as geographic targets change). The first step was to expand beyond our call center in San Francisco and place sales reps in the field. We needed individuals who were experts in the various markets and professionals with a proven track record. Although the corporate sales team did a fantastic job on the phone, they weren't the right group to build enterprise sales. They had just graduated from college, had no experience selling face-to-face, and wore T-shirts and jeans to work. They didn't even own suits and ties. (Not an anomaly in California, but not necessarily something that would translate across the country.)

We asked salesforce.com executive Carl Schachter, previously salesforce.com's VP of business development, to start the field sales team. In the very beginning, Carl was based in San Francisco, and the requirements of the job meant that he was constantly crisscrossing the country to deliver sales presentations. It wasn't efficient (and we soon based people in various cities), but this early step proved that enterprise clients placed a great importance on face-to-face meetings.

Conducting these in-person meetings also provided greater insight into what worked, and it offered us an opportunity to hone our sales pitch. Carl created two sales approaches. Pitch A embraced *practicality:* it highlighted the success of the product and its low risk, which made it a perfect solution in uncertain times. Pitch B evoked the *vision:* it introduced how the cloud computing model brought democracy to enterprise software and how it empowered customers. It tapped the innate desire to be a part of something that was new and exciting and urged people to join a revolution and participate in changing the world. (At the same time, of course, we had to include a message of utility and demonstrate that the product had real value.)

To decide which pitch to use, Carl invested time doing research about each prospect. That type of preparation made a huge difference. No matter what strategy we used, the number-one focus was on our customer's needs and providing a solution that could be implemented instantly. Unlike traditional enterprise software companies, we did not mention what could be done theoretically or what we could offer in the future. We focused on what could be achieved immediately.

Preparation Is Almost Everything

- Know the prospect's business and products.
- Understand the prospect's requirements.
- Predict any objections the prospect might have.
- Learn the business drivers of the prospect's success.

We developed a bifurcated strategy to grow sales. The corporate sales team, which conducted business mostly over the phone and via Web conferencing tools, was based at our headquarters in San Francisco. Having everyone in one place had proven to be a terrific way to build competition and camaraderie, and it also made it simple to deliver frequent training. This team targeted companies with fewer than five hundred employees. The field sales team approached the companies with more than five hundred employees. (We've since moved the line between corporate and field sales from five hundred employees to one thousand employees.)

Our goal was to create a balanced portfolio of small, medium, and large customers. Although we wanted to grow rapidly, we could not build a field sales team overnight. Instead, we grew strategically as necessary, segmenting the business according to geographic territories and business size. Our first domestic outpost was New York, where we hired A-list players from great companies to grow business on the East Coast. Later we added territories in Chicago and Atlanta.

We needed a leader to grow our worldwide sales and distribution effort. Jim Steele, the executive VP of worldwide sales at Ariba Corporation, came highly recommended by our executive search firm. Around the same time that we were recruiting Jim, we were separately (and without Jim's knowledge) recruiting one of his star players, David Rudnitsky. David's genius for selling to enterprise clients was matched only by his gift for picking game-changing start-up companies. (He'd worked at Oracle, Netscape, and Ariba, each in its earliest days.) After some convincing on my part, both signed on, and I was elated when David—who had won Netscape's first enterprise sale when McGraw-Hill bought ten thousand browsers all at once—made me an amazing promise: "I'll get you your first thousand-user deal."

Jim and David had been with us only for a week or two when an incredible opportunity unfolded at SunGard, a NYSE Fortune 1000 company. Cris Conde, who had just been promoted to CEO, was looking for a way to integrate the data systems giant's eighty different business units and saw CRM as the "unifying glue." The possibility of our biggest customer to date, and the thousand-user deal David had guaranteed, was right in front of us. At the time, SunGard's various divisions were working on myriad systems, but Cris noted that salesforce.com was the only one that was spreading virally. "The sales people were buying it on their own; they were swiping their own credit cards and going around their managers to purchase an account," he said.

That "vote" from the users was significant to Cris, and meeting with him to discuss our service's capabilities not only yielded our biggest customer at the time but also helped build a blueprint for selling to all enterprise companies. Cris shared with the sales team exactly what he needed, and we knew immediately that we were capable of providing these abilities to SunGard—or to any customer:

1. Security: data couldn't get leaked or lost.
2. Scalability: it had to grow with the company.
3. Reliability: it had to be accessible 24/7.
4. Performance: it had to work right away.
5. Integration: it had to integrate with the back-office systems.
6. Customization: it had to look and feel like a SunGard edition.

In addition, Cris stressed another demand: "We want the pay-as-you-go business model. It aligns your company's goals with our goals." As we entered into our biggest deal of that time, our subscription model became validated as something that won large and small customers alike.

The SunGard deal helped us land additional enterprise clients, and we soon learned another important lesson: We could no longer be driven solely by price. Simply being the cheapest wouldn't do anything for anyone. The service had to work as well as, or better than, the expensive versions if big customers were going to make a long-term switch.

Even our biggest customers reiterated this point. "I am not focused on how inexpensive it is; I am looking for value," Rick Justice, executive VP of worldwide operations and business development at Cisco, said. He didn't even want to talk about pricing until we proved the product's worth.

The Rudnitsky Sales Playbook

The best salespeople are driven by instinct, passion, and a powerful work ethic. Ultimately, though, closing great deals always comes down to execution. David initially created this playbook for the global financial services division, which he runs, but it proved so successful that it has been deployed throughout our entire enterprise sales team. Some of the following ideas may not be revolutionary, but it's uncommon for salespeople to actually employ all of them. If they do internalize these ideas and execute them, they will find success. Guaranteed.

Think BIG, Have Attitude

Think big when strategizing with your customers, and focus on their entire potential enterprise needs, not just the immediate opportunity in front of you. Think big (dollars and scope) when delivering a proposal to your customers. Get them excited and emotionally connected to the bigger vision. Think bigger than any opportunity of the past.

Similarly, behave as if your company is big, even if it's not. When David and Jim started, our biggest customer had five hundred users. Our average customer had twelve users. We shared this information, but we *focused* on where our company was headed, and how right now — as the industry was transforming and we were ushering in the future — was the right time to buy.

No Deal Is Won or Lost Alone

Every deal should be touched by multiple people. Trust the people around you and divide and conquer. "I'm less impressed with someone who closes a $2 million deal alone than I am with someone who brought all of us in and still closed the same $2 million deal," says David. At a minimum, bringing in the rest of the team helps mitigate risk and, in most cases, helps sell more. Our enterprise team regularly holds "account challenges" where account executives present the deals they are working on and brainstorm about what they want to accomplish and the potential challenges.

Connect the Dots

Don't dial for dollars! Never cold-call; always call with a plan. Learn about the company and use your network to find the right individual(s) to approach. Our sales team uses our network the same way people use the business networking Web site LinkedIn, constantly reaching out to our contacts (our executive team or our board of directors) to find connections. With the reach of our executives, customers, and partners, it is almost impossible not to be able somehow to connect the dots before engaging with a prospect. When we were trying to win lender CIT as a customer, for example, we realized that Gary Butler, the CEO of ADP, a customer of ours, was on the board of CIT. I reached out to Gary, who recommended us to CIT. The first meeting we had at CIT was with its CEO and chairman, Jeffrey Peek. By connecting the dots, we won the unlikely opportunity to get to the "C" level on an initial sales call. This ultimately resulted in a multithousand-user deal and an extremely short sales cycle.

Focus on "Why Not"

Everyone wants to think about why a deal will close, but it's more prudent to focus on why it might not. Think about the five or six things that could be problematic. Then figure out how to solve those problems in advance. Focusing on the "Whys" puts you at best on par with your competitors; anticipating the "Why nots" gives you a significant advantage over them.

Always Take the Deal off the Table

If a deal is ready, close it. This eliminates such risks as the buyer leaving his job or the market tanking. We recently got the sense that a multimillion-dollar deal was stalling. We did everything to create a sense of urgency and get the deal signed. It was a good thing we did: two weeks later the CIO, who was also our executive sponsor, left the company, but not before our contract was executed. We could have continued to negotiate for a larger deal, but getting the deal off the table proved to be far more valuable.

Get Your Face in the Place

You can't learn everything about your customers over the phone. Walk their halls — frequently. It strengthens a customer's confidence in you and establishes a rapport.

Fun Facts Build Instant Credibility

Know all you can about how other customers are specifically using your product. Know which departments of a company you might already be in, who you are working with, who you beat out, and why. Collect a "fun facts" library and use this information to build credibility with prospects.

Be Proactive on All Paperwork

Don't get caught in the momentum of the deal and avoid the paperwork. It will come back to bite you.

Always Get Quid Pro Quo in Negotiations

Great salespeople have the confidence to say no. Always consider what else you can get before you say yes. Ask for more users, a certain close date, or a press release about the deal. Revealing new deals in the press, such as the signing of SunGard, allowed us to get the word out and get our foot in the door with other financial institutions and enterprise clients. Winning SunGard validated our service as reliable and secure, and directly helped us close our next enterprise deal, with the HR and payroll services giant ADP. (Terms surrounding disclosure about the agreement must be penned in the deal: make certain you can announce the win, including why the company is using your service and whom you beat, but ensure that numbers cannot be disclosed.)

Share Best Practices

Celebrate successes — and learn from them. Send the great e-mails and great proposals to the rest of the team so that they can see what's worked and use them in other deals.

Go After Game Changers

Pursue deals that help move the company to the next level. These deals are revolutionary in a company's evolution. They redefine how a company sells, evolve the sales model, and challenge everyone to get to the next level. Winning huge customers, such as Dell and Japan Post, was game changing for our company.

Play #47: Land and Expand

We began with eighty users at ADP and seventy-five users at Merrill Lynch; both initial deals scaled to multithousand-user commitments once we were in the door and after we had the opportunity to prove our service. We learned that when you are starting out, you can't try to capture an entire company at once. Start in a small division. Companies are looking to limit their investment risk, and they appreciate an opportunity to take a smaller position, experience the benefits, and then make additional purchases. This marks a fundamental shift from the process of the traditional software industry, which tries to bag entire organizations in one go. In the end, "land and expand" achieves that same goal, but also makes it possible for newer businesses to win larger or more established customers.

Once there's success with a few departments, you are well positioned for an enterprise-wide purchase and deployment commitment. Recommend a corporate license agreement spanning departments and multiple products. The pitch: it's less expensive than gradual adoption at list price, and it's easier to deploy.

From "Try and Buy" to "Buy and Try"

We started out with a free trial: five free subscriptions a year. This nourished our seed-and-grow strategy to first serve small companies and smaller departments within larger companies. As

---

Play #48: Abandon Strategies That No Longer Serve You

As we grew distribution, we soon discovered that some of the strategies that had proven successful in the past no longer made sense as we evolved. A perfect example was the free trials, which had previously been so essential to our success. A few months into our effort to win enterprise clients, Frank van Veenendaal came to me concerned that the free trial—and the low barrier to entry—was doing us a disservice.

Frank believed that customers weren't thinking as carefully about their salesforce.com implementation as they would had it required a larger investment. He found that users weren't conducting appropriate due diligence and weren't striving to win the support of their executive committees. The absence of that buy-in had an adverse effect on customer success—and on our business.

"In 10 to 15 percent of cases, a salesforce.com user would hear, 'I didn't approve that,'" Frank told me. He urged that we up the ante as a way to generate more support for our service. I knew he was right: it was time to stop selling salesforce.com as a solution that was inexpensive enough to be purchased every month and slipped by on an individual's expense report.

we scaled to close enterprise-wide deals, we set up a paid trial that allowed customers to "buy and try" our service before committing to a large purchase. Both of these early trials won initial adoption — and yielded larger deployment later.

Instead of sneaking in under the radar, we needed to respect organizational hierarchy.

One of the changes we made was the introduction of a more complex trial—a proof of concept that demonstrated to larger companies that we could customize the solution to their needs. In acknowledgment of the increased costs of building more complex trials and our desire for a greater investment from users, we evolved the free trial to a "buy and try" experience. We found that with skin in the game on both sides, we were able to connect more easily with the appropriate business and technical constituents and win organization-wide support.

Play #49: Old Customers Need Love

Although companies must always be on a quest for new customers, they can never forget about existing customers. We built a customer success managers (CSM) organization to ensure that current customers continued with our service. The SaaS model makes it easy for customers to churn if they are not successful, for unlike the on-premise model, it doesn't force customers into taking on excessive up-front costs and technical infrastructure changes.

Because we can see if the users are logging on to the Salesforce application (it's running on our computers), we know that if a customer is not logging on, he or she is not achieving success and will therefore almost certainly leave us at the end of contract. Our CSM team visits these customers, finds the problems, and fixes them for free. The CSM organization works: renewal rates at salesforce.com have been about 90 percent (and that includes customers who go out of business).

Play #50: Add It On and Add It Up

As we won wider adoption within organizations and won new enterprise clients, we found that we had to change the way we promoted the "do-it-yourself" aspect of the installation. Our service designed for large corporations was more robust, and these customers, especially when embarking on a very large implementation, were seeking and expecting more formal guidance than we had previously offered. To meet this need, we focused on building a professional services group. The new division made sense on various levels: it helped customers get the most out of the service; it offered an opportunity for us to disseminate our expertise; and it provided an add-on product to sell. (Sales reps receive additional commission for selling professional services.)

It made sense for us to extend our offering with a professional services division, which allowed us to build a world-class sales team and serve customers more effectively. It was always our objective to make every customer feel as if he or she were the only one with whom we were working, and this division helped us meet that goal.

I've always made myself very accessible to customers. Everyone has my e-mail address (ceo@salesforce.com), and I can assure you that people use it. I answer every customer e-mail I receive.

If I hear from the CEO of a company with one subscription who says that he or she is disappointed with the service, I immediately respond and say that someone from professional services will be in touch. (I copy professional services on the e-mail and ask the customer to follow up with me and let me know how it goes.) This approach works: the situation is usually resolved in a few minutes, and I frequently receive very happy e-mails from customers.

There is an important part of professional services that partners with outside organizations such as Accenture, KPMG, Deloitte, and other consultancies that recommend and help enable our service. We've had great success partnering with these organizations to win customers. This strategy was not possible when we first started, but as salesforce.com and the industry matures, it makes more sense. It's exciting to see other consulting firms selling and helping deploy our services. In fact, one of salesforce.com's earliest hires, Mitch Wallace, now works for a new company, Veeva Systems, which implements our service, and Eric Berridge, who worked for me at Oracle, started Bluewolf Group as an on-demand consultancy to serve this need as well.

It's exciting to have played a part in launching new businesses, and we eagerly welcome these partners into our ecosystem as they help us sell our service and grow. At the same time, we are still investing in our internal services team. In fact, the demand for salesforce.com tech-heads is greater than ever, and we've morphed our team into an expert services corps. Even with the relationships with other firms, we've found that many companies, such as Dell, demand a saleforce.com presence. Some of them, like IT industry veteran Bob Ridout, the former CIO of DuPont, specifically demanded my presence. Ultimately, we must do whatever it takes to ensure that customers are successful.

We have to because that's what drives renewals, but understanding the value of making customers successful is a lesson that all companies can relate to.

Play #51: Success Is the Number One Selling Feature

When we started salesforce.com, companies sold separate software systems to small, medium, and large companies. We wanted to change that and provide everyone with the same affordable and effective service. For as long as I can remember, people told us we couldn't serve all markets—they told us that it could not be done.

Admittedly, our evolution did not always unfold as we originally envisioned it, but our seed-and-grow strategy proved effective across the board. It made sense to start with small companies, which validated our service to larger organizations. As we grew our product line to serve enterprise businesses, it similarly made sense to start small within the larger institutions. It's amazing to consider that no matter what size customer we were pitching, or where in the world we were selling, a singular idea drove all our accomplishments: we never sold features. We sold the model and we sold the customer's success. Today, one-third of our revenue is from small business, one-third from medium business, and one-third from large companies, including Cisco, E*TRADE Financial, and Starbucks.

Our best customers have become our best salespeople. After we proved the value of our service to Dell, for example, it introduced us to its top two vendors, who are now customers. The most effective thing you can do to sell your product is to introduce a prospect to a happy customer. Happy customers are the strongest troops in the most powerful sales army.

Metrics Used to Monitor Success

These are some metrics that you can use to measure your sales team's success. Knowing these metrics helps the sales organization predict revenue and build a financial plan:

- Inbound sales
- Raw Web traffic
- Capture rate
- Lead conversion rate
- Close rate
- Average deal size
- Percentage of business that is from new customers as opposed to customers that are adding on (If you are adding on more than you are closing, there won't be anything to add on next year.)
- Sales cycle length
- Sales productivity (the average amount the sales rep closed on a monthly basis)

PART 5

The Technology Playbook
How to Develop Products Users Love

Play #52: Have the Courage to Pursue Your Innovation—Before It Is Obvious to the Market

I came up with the idea about how to build salesforce.com in my sleep. Literally. I had a weird dream in which I envisioned Amazon.com, but instead of the tabs with Books, CDs, or DVDs, they said Accounts, Contacts, Opportunities, Forecasts, and Reports. After this dream, I had an almost crystal-clear picture of where we were going. The words of Walt Disney rang in my mind: "If you can dream it, you can do it." That said, I had no idea how we were going to get there.

Everything rested on inventing the technology to enable an Internet-based business service that could be used simultaneously by masses of people. Salesforce.com creates a lot of noise with its guerilla marketing stunts, but the engine that really drives our company—the one effort that our success wholly relies on—is producing a service that customers love. The extravagant parties wouldn't be enthusiastically attended, the gonzo tactics wouldn't be consistently reported, and the salespeople wouldn't be receiving their commissions if we were not offering a service that delivered everything we promised.

Historically, companies such as Oracle approached development by thinking of designing for the biggest companies in the world. Systems were built on individual stacks of software and hardware capable of scaling to manage information for the entire staff of General Motors or all of General Electric. That was a tall order, but we were doing much more. We were designing a single service to manage information for all the companies in the world to use at the same time.

To design a limitless system, we had to think differently about software design. As Parker Harris liked to say, "We had to build it from the ground up for the Internet." The service would be one logical system 100 percent hosted by salesforce.com, which would scale dynamically as subscribers and new customers adopted the service. That presented benefits for customers, such as sharing common capabilities (IT assets like database engines, disk space, and security), which would reduce risks and costs. At the same time, each customer received a securely partitioned, highly personalized experience with their own data, logic, and end-user experience.

We call this technology model "multitenancy," and it's easy to think of it as an apartment building where the tenants of the building share common costs, such as building security or the laundry facilities, but they still have locks on their doors and the freedom to decorate their apartments as they wish. Consumer services like Yahoo! Mail or Microsoft's Hotmail use this kind of model—it's how their consumers access their individual mail accounts cheaply (or even for free) through a browser without the need to install any software and how millions of users share the same back-end systems. These companies don't set up a new e-mail server for each consumer. Similarly, we thought business application providers didn't need to set up a new server for each customer when there was the possibility for everyone to share it.

Although we believed that this technology model was a way to reduce the operational burdens for customers, our SaaS concept, by which a customer handed over his or her proprietary data to be housed on our server—and then "rented" access to our software—sounded like lunacy to most people.

We heard the same concern over and over again: a panic over giving up control. I believed that the trepidation was more emotional than rational, but it led to pressure to offer another option. Venture capitalists argued that we should build a technology model that accommodated a choice: a hosted model to lure in smaller businesses, and an "in-house" packaged software option similar to what was being offered by the traditional companies for larger companies.

No way, we decided. Although hedging a bet might be prudent in some cases, our idea simply couldn't work if we offered a choice. Doing so would ruin everything. To truly benefit from the on-demand model, our customers all had to be using one version so that when we did maintenance and upgrades—benefits that the technology model allowed us to do continuously—everyone would receive the same features automatically. (In the in-house model, users are never on the most current version. It's such a nuisance to upgrade, in fact, that even SAP, which has teams of people to coerce customers to install its latest software, reportedly doesn't always run on its own most recent technology!)

There was also a philosophical reason that we couldn't offer a hosted choice. We believed in the End of Software—that all companies would eventually use the Internet to replace all the software they once installed on PCs. This was our religion. How could we promote the very software option we were trying to destroy? As we went against conventional wisdom, we found the secret to being successful in the technology industry. Companies must not only see innovation before it is obvious to the market but also have the courage to pursue that innovation years before it's accepted, or even understood.

Play #53: Invest in the Long Term with a Prototype That Sets a Strong Foundation

In the earliest days of salesforce.com, our small team believed that our idea could work, but we had no real sense of how far we could take it. How much could we scale the service? How many users could we have on the system? How could we make it infinite?

Our philosophy was to write code that lasted for the long haul. Practically on day one, Parker, Dave, and Frank developed their own guiding principles about the system: "Do it fast, simple, and right the first time (and did we mention fast?)." They wrote these "laws" on a white board, and they stuck. They forced us to create code that was simple and efficient, and this is what ultimately gave us the ability to scale.

Doing it fast makes sense as the number-one rule for any company. It was particularly critical for us because we were selling a service for salespeople: they need information quickly and tend to be impatient. Being fast became a proof point for the model; if it wasn't fast, people weren't going to use it.

Our second law, to make it simple, supported our vision to make our service as easy to use as buying a book on Amazon.com. Simplicity also supported our first goal to keep it fast. A typical programmer at this time had the mind-set that big and robust code was beautiful. We didn't agree; complicated code becomes bloated and slow. We aspired to trim the code to be as minimal as possible. That type of architecture also made it easier to identify any problems as we scaled.

When it came to our goal of doing it right the first time, we knew there was no other way. Software development is incredibly complex. There's great pressure to get a prototype out and to cut corners in order to meet deadlines. Parker, Dave, Frank, and I had witnessed how shortcuts sparked major issues later. We knew that the initial prototype set the foundation for the entire product. If it's messy out of the gate, it can't hold up over time. In fact, it's common for the code to explode as developers try to transition and scale. These so-called success disasters have plagued the software industry. They don't have to.

Play #54: Follow the Lead of Companies That Are Loved by Their Customers

The development model that we embraced was different from the one with which we were accustomed to working in the corporate America of the 1990s. Enterprise software had traditionally been built by engineers who worked in corporate office parks with little or no interaction with the customers until a pre-determined "five-year plan" was complete. This isolationist existence had seriously stymied innovation in the technology industry. Companies were not moving fast enough for customers.

Consumer companies, such as Google, eBay, and Yahoo!, were the first to change the pace. The developers at those companies didn't go MIA for several years and then suddenly roll out everything they'd been working on at once. These companies launched a single application (Google and Yahoo! started with search, eBay with auctions) and then feverishly built out a product suite after they evaluated how the application was being used. It involved a process that took weeks instead of years. Delivering a service over the Internet offered a more evolved and more efficient way to observe usage and engage with customers that we believed would define the entire future of software engineering.

Although each of the salesforce.com founders had a lot of ambition and energy, we knew the biggest threat to a fledgling technology company is doing too much at once. Our ultimate goal was to have a comprehensive line of products to serve everyone, but it didn't make sense to kick off with a suite of services, or editions specifically geared to different-sized businesses. It would have taken years and endless funding to build something so complex, and by the time we released it, we would have missed the real opportunity to capture a piece of the market. Worst of all, we would have been designing in a vacuum, without the benefit of our customers' invaluable observations and insights to guide us as we built each new feature.

Play #55: Don't Do It All Yourself; Reuse, Don't Rebuild

When it came to building innovative technology, we took a bet on a few existing things. First, we took a big bet on the Internet, and on Java as the programming language for the Internet. Second, we relied on the Oracle database. Oracle's database was large and fast, and we were familiar with it, so there was no reason to build our own. There were less expensive options, but we were not as confident that the other solutions would be able to scale. Today, our back end is still a giant Oracle database that we customize for each tenant and where they can continuously update their data.

The secret to building winning technology was not only that we bet on the right building blocks but also that our vendors' executives were personally committed to our success. Today, more than ever before, companies do not need to build technology from scratch; you can build on Internet-based platforms and tap into distribution centers, data centers, and unlimited computing power. The cloud computing model saves time and capital. All companies benefit when they can afford to focus on innovation rather than infrastructure.

Consider Appirio, a software and services company that runs its entire business in the cloud. It has exploded from zero to one hundred fifty people in twenty-three states and in three countries in two-and-a-half years—and spent less than one-third of what a company of its size spends on IT. "Because of the cloud we were able to save money and be more innovative in how we work," says cofounder and marketing chief Narinder

Singh. "We're like a next-generation IBM without the baggage of hardware."

Play #56: Embrace Transparency and Build Trust

One of the biggest issues for any cloud computing company is ensuring reliability of the service. We had made massive efforts to ensure that our service would always be up, such as configuring our database to run on several different servers so that if one machine failed, the others would still work, yet in late 2005 our site went down. Customers quickly began to grumble that the service was unreliable. Making matters worse, a competitor signed up for a free trial as a way to ascertain when our service was down—and reported any problems to the press. Literally, within minutes, journalists would call seeking comment. Before long, salesforce.com's reliability issues were widely publicized, and we were in serious trouble.

During the period we struggled with outages, we actually had an uptime rate of 99 percent, and our service was much better and much more reliable than software, but any disruption was understandably maddening for customers. We lost their faith.

Salesforce.com entered an incredibly challenging time. There were fundamental issues with our technology model, and it was unclear whether or not we'd be able to go forward on our current code base. We questioned if the technology would be able to scale as much as it needed to, and whether or not we would be able to continue to deliver the same level of innovation.

Parker and the team of engineers tirelessly scrambled to fix the problem by working with our vendors at Oracle, Sun, and Veritas and rebuilding the software and executing myriad stability projects. We dedicated all our technology resources to solving this issue. All development on new features temporarily stopped. As the engineers worked around the clock to find a solution, the rest of us were unsure of how to respond to the escalating criticism. No one knew what to say to customers or to the press, but we believed a strategy of minimization and containment would serve us best.

At the time, I felt that our public response was not our primary concern. I thought we needed to focus on improving the technology and to remain as low profile as possible until the problem was resolved. Once everything was fixed, I thought, we could respond with a proper explanation and share good news. We stopped taking calls, and we stopped returning calls. This seemed like the safe response, but it was unlike the way salesforce.com usually operated, which made us feel uncomfortable.

"This is not who we are; we are usually the ones calling people up," Bruce Francis, the vice president of corporate strategy, said to me one day during the height of the crisis. "Hiding doesn't feel right."

I had to admit that part of me felt that if we didn't confirm the problems, they didn't exist. I had mistakenly assumed that reporters wouldn't write about the issues if they didn't have our comment. That was an antiquated assumption, however. Blogging was just taking off, and bloggers don't adhere to the traditional rules that magazine or newspaper reporters follow, such as holding a story until they get confirmation or comment. After the blogs covered it, the established media picked it up.

We realized that silence had been a terrible strategy. And it wasn't just the decision not to talk that had been an egregious error, it was that we had not talked immediately. Part of the problem was exacerbated by the very nature of SaaS: because we hosted everything, people couldn't call their own data centers and learn what was happening. Customers were annoyed.

As the crisis built, we gathered our top two hundred fifty managers at an offsite meeting. The reliability of our service was, of course, the most pressing topic. Right then we had our worst outage to date. The system went down, and restarting the huge databases took ninety minutes—an eternity for customers dependent on the service. Customers and the press were clamoring for answers, and it was difficult for them to reach anyone because all our managers were at the off-site meeting.

We had to find a way to communicate quickly and candidly—even if going public with our problems felt like a defeat at the moment. Parker and Bruce urged me to post our internal monitoring system, which we used to track our status (everything running perfectly appeared in green, performance issues were tagged in yellow, and service disruptions were marked in red). It was a bold move and a big leap of faith. We would be allowing the public—and the competition—to see exactly how our system was functioning every day. It meant that we would be sharing embarrassing details every time the system slowed or stopped working. Why would any company make itself vulnerable in that way?

At first I was hesitant. It made sense that customers would see what was going on in real time, but I didn't think that our reliability information should be available to everybody. I worried that journalists and our competitors would use this information against us. Ultimately, however, I let go of my fear and realized that complete transparency was what we needed if we were to restore trust in our company. It would also encourage good behavior from the organization because it added a new level of accountability and responsibility. In the middle of the disaster, we opened up our internal system for everyone to see. I called it the trust site.

The site—located at trust.salesforce.com—offers real-time information on system performance with up-to-the minute information on planned maintenance, historical information on transaction volume and speed, reports on current and recent phishing and malware attempts, and information on new security technologies and the best security practices. Instead of hiding behind our problems, we started educating customers, prospects, and journalists about where they could find the information they needed. It was liberating not to have to act defensively.

The effort was an instant hit with reporters as they could immediately see for themselves what was happening. We further benefited because it took the "gotcha" weapon away from competitors. Best of all, the trust site gave us an opportunity to talk about something positive—transparency.

There is no question: we would not be around today if we were not always bettering the technology and improving its speed and reliability. (Our service ran at 99.99 percent uptime in the first quarter of 2009, runs more than 200 million transactions a day, and has subsecond response time; and we are constantly making advances to deliver it even faster.) At the same time, I don't think we would be thriving today had we not shifted to embrace more transparency. The difficult decision to launch the trust site—to "open the kimono," as Bruce Francis called it—differentiated us. Transparency and trust became a strong part of our branding and identity.

Reliability Is a Tech Problem, but the Way You Solve It Is Not with Technology Alone—It's with Communication

Once again, we did not invent this solution; we got our inspiration from the consumer world: eBay pioneered this idea with its pages that inform users of outages, glitches, and maintenance upgrades. This had not been done in the corporate world before we did it, though it has since been validated as a best practice for companies of all stripes. When BlackBerry struggled with service outages, many articles pointed to the salesforce.com trust site as a way to deal successfully with these issues. Out of a crisis that had threatened to damage our reputation, we had created powerful differentiation. Now, we talk about transparency in every pitch we make to the press and to prospective customers. It's a cornerstone of our messaging.

Today, if our servers are down — even for twenty minutes — we call our top customers. I call many of our customers personally to apologize and share what is happening. Often they are completely surprised to hear from me. One CIO at a very large company told me that he couldn't believe I was taking the time to call him. He revealed that he had had data centers down for two days, so an hour of downtime didn't represent a massive problem to him. We found, however, that open communication, in tandem with quickly fixing the problem, is the only way to build and retain trust.

Play #57: Let Your Customers Drive Innovation

We aimed to make the salesforce.com service similar to the consumer Web sites that people had already embraced. We wanted customers to love to use the Salesforce application, so we started by giving them something they were familiar with: tabs across the top of a Web page. Initially, as I saw in my dream, we had five tabs: Contacts, Accounts, Opportunities, Forecasts, and Reports. These tabs represented the five things that our company did. The application was much simpler than the existing enterprise software packages, but even without all the bells and whistles, it enabled customers to turn opportunities into deals.

From the very beginning, we initiated a dialogue with these users about what was missing in the Sales Force Automation (SFA) application. Salespeople routinely asked prospects about features they wanted and relayed their feedback to the product managers. We queried prospects on why they decided *not* to go with us, and we spent time with large enterprises—customers that we weren't initially able to serve—to learn what additional functionality was required to make them consider our service. We heard about missing features, such as the ability to track multiple products or a way to manage price lists. We might have thought of these on our own, or we might not have, but we certainly wouldn't have known which were in the greatest demand.

Thanks to our "no software" model, we have another way to listen to customer response. The on-demand architecture offers us the opportunity to "watch" how users use the application. We don't do this in a Big Brother way, where we can see data or information about a company. Rather, the system simply counts broad patterns anonymously and notifies us if there are issues.

These insights into how users are using our service allows us to learn about what they use and what they don't.

As we evolved our service in response to customers' needs, we faced the risk of changing our service too much—and making it so specific that it couldn't commonly serve all customers. If we wanted to continue to have mass appeal, we needed to apply changes with a broad brush.

It wasn't long before we began to notice fairly consistent feedback that the initial five tabs were not enough for all customers. There were two fundamental ways in which we could have expanded. One was vertical, meaning that we could make the existing tabs go deeper with increased functionality (such as pharmaceutical or banking); the other way was horizontal, or going broader with additional tabs (for example, Case Management, Solutions, or Documents).

We ultimately made the decision to do both. Although we needed to limit our expansion to ensure that we did not spread ourselves too thin, we had to recognize our goal to be the on-demand market leader. If we wanted to achieve that, we needed to have the capacity to serve both the small business and large business markets.

The limitless potential of the Internet allowed us to build this capacity, and the ideas for the changes we made came directly from customers and prospects. We launched only what they requested, and we considered their insights, even when we didn't agree. That was one of our wisest moves. Looking back, we now know that our biggest evolutionary epiphany stemmed from a customer request—one that we initially believed was impractical and that we were reluctant to pursue.

After we had been offering our service for a few years, a health care executive called me and complained about how the salesforce.com tabs were labeled. "The tab names don't speak to our people," said Marty Howard, Senior VP at Patient Care. "I have 'hospitals'; I don't have 'accounts.' I have 'patients'; I don't have 'contacts.'"

"Just think of the hospital as an account and think of the patient as a contact—it's simple," I said.

"No, that's too confusing," Marty replied. "Why can't you just rename the tabs? I think it's important for other companies and other industries as well."

Rename the tabs? To be honest, this seemed ridiculous— the tabs had general words like Contacts, which from a high level applied to most users. We couldn't change it just for one person.

We decided that Marty deserved for us at least to consider his request, and as we thought about it more critically, we stumbled on another idea. What if we didn't change the tabs for one person, but rather let everyone change the tabs? What if we left the tabs blank and offered a way for customers to type in tab names that directly corresponded to their line of work? Car services could track "drivers" and "vehicles." A recruiter could manage "positions" and "prospective employees." Nonprofits could follow "causes" and "donors." This change would allow us to provide every user with a customized experience, and it would potentially extend our reach. I became captivated by this idea, and I called the developers to meet with me to discuss how to build it.

"We'll do it, but it's tedious," Parker and Dave complained.

"Let's just figure out how to do it," I suggested.

"It will have ramifications that will cascade through the whole product line," Dave warned.

"Yes, I think it will be a key feature of the technology," I replied. I wasn't afraid of this game change; I was excited about it. Dave spent one month creating a way for customers to customize the tabs to their individual needs. The new capability was immediately met with huge applause. It made the application more relevant to users—and it made salesforce.com stickier.

Our decision to add tabs had been an exciting part of our evolution, but it was the blank tabs that were revolutionary. Responding to customer demand, we expanded from renaming tabs to including the possibility of renaming fields, and eventually to creating new fields. These new custom objects allowed companies to incorporate additional information that would specifically serve them. Hospitals could create custom objects to track medical instruments and their locations. A recruiting company could create a place to track a prospective employee's past experience, and another object to manage interview schedules. We also added a workflow section, which allowed users to store information—for example, a place where a recruiter could direct resumes or where a sales manager could create a task to send out an e-mail whenever a $1 million deal was closed.

With each of these available customization features, users were able to create mini applications customized to their needs. The capability was designed so that customization could be executed through the use of drop-down menus and point-and-click configuration tools, without having to write a line of code. As our customers became involved in customizing features to suit their needs, we gained even more salesforce.com enthusiasts. We moved users from adoption to addiction.

Play #58: Make It Easy for Customers to Adopt

We made a significant leap in the technology when we offered integration capabilities by providing an application programming interface (API), or a way for salesforce.com to communicate with other programs. This transformed our product and technology so that the data in salesforce.com were not isolated in Web silos, but could interact with other data that were behind the firewall or on other Web sites. The API, for example, allowed salesforce.com to interface with Google Maps, so salespeople could instantly access a map of where all their customers were located. Google and salesforce.com "talked" through the API. Salesforce.com provided all the information, and Google generated the balloons on the map. This move to allow integration was a giant step in our evolution.

Early on, we struggled with a way to explain the API. We knew it was important, but SaaS wasn't truly an accepted concept yet, and our API was initially confusing. Further, we made the mistake of limiting availability by charging a significant fee and restricting its use to companies with proven revenue. We realized that those barriers made adoption difficult. In an effort to get more support, we went back to our proven strategy of first offering access to a new service for free. We also started an online forum for people to ask questions, which offered us a way to build a community.

Providing easier accessibility and additional educational opportunities proved to be the right move. Before long, there were more users, more activity, and more transactions moving through the Web services API than there were through the application.

Play #59: Transcend Technical Paradigms

One of the most pivotal decisions we made as a company was to make our code available to let other companies build their own complementary online services. This idea to become a platform, or an operating system for the Internet (similar to how Windows is an operating system for PCs), offered a way to allow everyone to create applications online and gave us an opportunity to attract and retain more customers. This was the way to grow our company.

Despite my bullish belief in Platform-as-a-Service (PaaS), the decision of whether or not to go ahead with the idea was a daunting one. Could we build an Internet operating system? There were potentially gigantic compatibility risks involved in allowing someone else's code to operate on our system. We didn't even know if customers would trust it. It wasn't surprising that there wasn't much internal support for such an untested idea.

However, creating a platform offered a way to resolve our biggest problem: customers were clamoring for more applications, and we didn't have the resources to build everything ourselves. Further, we knew that outside developers needed a better way to create applications. There was so much that was truly painful about the process, and the heavy lifting required to build salesforce.com was fresh in my mind. There were so many decisions and purchases: networking devices, storage systems, databases, open source databases, data centers. And those were only the start-up software considerations! Then we had to build the software and make sure it worked in multiple languages and on multiple devices, among other challenges. After that, there were technology issues to address, such as authentication and availability.

I wondered why everyone in the industry put themselves through this onerous process when, with the benefits of multitenancy, those days could be over. We could make everything much less complex and far less expensive by sharing our resources.

There was a huge audience of developers, especially those in emerging countries who couldn't afford to build according to the current model. If we could make our infrastructure available as a service, we could help level the playing field—and, I thought, unleash innovation. The "platform in the cloud" effort became a pet project of mine. Part of my drive stemmed from the intellectual challenge and my eagerness to innovate. The rest came from the potential the platform had to transform salesforce.com from an SFA application to a massive Web services company.

I hired Steve Fisher, a great technologist and my former business partner at Liberty Software, the company we founded in high school. Steve was confident that he could build such a platform, but he didn't necessarily like the conditions that I felt were required. I did not want Steve to be polluted by anything related to CRM, so I called his work a "secret project" and didn't allow anyone to talk to him.

Steve complained that he was lonely, but his complete focus and attention elicited quick results. In one week, he built the first application on the platform, Volunteerforce, which our employees still use to manage their volunteer activities. It did not take long before Steve created a way for users to toggle from salesforce.com into other applications, such as e-mail or spreadsheets, through the use of a drop-down menu. Some saw this simply as a pull-down menu, but I saw this capability to work with multiple applications as the beginning of a Web-based operating system.

With this tool, which we marketed (and called Multiforce), we began to segue salesforce.com into a platform for others to build on. Although some users liked the ability to customize without any code, larger and more tech-savvy users began to demand more complex customizations. We realized that the tools we used internally were valuable to other people too. We made our own native programming language, Apex, which we used to created new products, available to these developers. With this offering, they could write their own code and create and run any application on our platform, as well as use our other resources, such as our data center and security technology.

Through a technology Parker built called Visualforce, users could create any application with any user interface (for example, they could build any forms, create any buttons or links, and embed any mash-up). This feature took us far beyond the original concept of allowing users to "rename the tabs." In fact, users could get rid of my beloved tabs that had once defined everything we did! The technology offered a way for developers to build on a blank page and opened up a new world of possibilities. Users could create any interface design they desired. They gained the ability to run that user interface on any Internet-enabled device or operating system platform, so it could appear in one format when viewed on an iPhone and in another format when viewed on Safari or Mozilla or even a touch-based kiosk.

We saw PaaS as the natural extension of the SaaS business model. We ultimately branded the salesforce.com platform as Force.com. At first, as we had anticipated, customers were apprehensive to build on it. We got calls from people asking, "Am I going to break your computers with my code?" We had, of course, figured out a way to prevent that. Our customers and partners have embraced PaaS and dramatically extended our scope with the creation of more than one hundred ten thousand custom applications managing everything from vacation requests to accounts receivable.

Some of the world's largest organizations, such as Citigroup, adopted Force.com to build programs used by private bankers and financial advisers. Morgan Stanley used it to build a recruiting application. International multimedia news powerhouse Thomson Reuters standardized on our platform and then implemented an entire strategy to sell products that are based on our platform. Japan Post, the world's largest institution in terms of asset holdings, used the platform to write customer service and regulatory compliance software for more than seventy thousand employees.

Other organizations have found innovative uses and benefits as well. Schumacher Group, a $300 million emergency department and hospital medicine management company in Lafayette, Louisiana, used our platform to build 90 percent of its operational applications, including programs to recruit doctors, get reimbursed by insurers, manage contracts, and assist in disaster response. Force.com allowed the company to write applications four times faster than conventional programs. It also saved significant resources. "If we weren't using the Force.com platform, we'd have to hire an additional five full-time employees to manage the system," chief information officer Douglas Menefee said in an interview with Bloomberg.com. The article noted that the salaries for those jobs range from $40,000 to

$80,000.[1] (Note: Great technology yields successful customers, which is what drives great press!)

The first decade of salesforce.com was dedicated to building a killer application to replace expensive shelfware. We grew our service to meet our customers' demands and expanded beyond SFA to include marketing, customer service, content management, analytics, and much more. We added mobile capabilities and borrowed ideas from social networking sites to allow our customers to communicate easily with each other and with us.

Our customers became better customers with each of these developments. Seagate Technology, for example, saw user adoption increase by 50 percent and extended how it used our service. We launched a "channel" component to allow our manufacturing customers to collaborate and share account information and leads with their corporate resellers, systems integrators, and other partners. For some companies, as much as 70 percent of their business is conducted through partner or channel sales, and they desperately needed a way to gain a 360-degree view across all their sales channels. This additional functionality allowed us to win customers that never looked at us before, such as Avaya. By giving customers what they needed, we were able to grow our business substantially and take it in a new direction.

The second decade of salesforce.com, which I think is even more exciting, focuses on PaaS, which allows customers to run all their enterprise applications and their Web sites and intranets in the cloud. By enabling developers to create and deliver any kind of business application, entirely on-demand and without software, salesforce.com has catapulted beyond its CRM roots and expanded into a multicategory company. New functionality has been built by our users and outside developers. For example, CODA, a financial managements solutions company in Europe, used our platform to create an accounting system that works with salesforce.com.

If CODA approached this the old way, by building the infrastructure (not just the data center but the entire software stack as well), it would have taken upwards of $20 million and several years. Using our platform eradicated the need for servers, load balancers, and networking switches and for people to tune and maintain them, and afforded CODA the luxury to focus on exactly what it does best: building a killer accounting application.

Play #60: Provide a Marketplace for Solutions

As new technology models evolved and as companies reached a point of having to decide which path to choose, the old PC model or cloud computing, we needed to do everything in our power to ensure that they selected the technology of the future.

We needed to make people aware of the amazing developments, so we decided to create an on-demand marketplace that packaged and distributed applications. We called the marketplace AppExchange and set it up as a single site where developers could upload applications they built, and customers could search, read reviews, test for free, and ultimately purchase and download new applications.

BusinessWeek called it the "eBay for business software," and *Forbes* described it as the "iTunes of business software." AppExchange—much like eBay and iTunes—works because communities work best with market dynamics. Like any other marketplace, we offered an opportunity for customers to find what they were looking for, an ability to test it, and a place to talk about it with other like-minded people. The upshot of this exchange was an incredible customer base for the developers who uploaded their applications—and a fantastic opportunity for salesforce.com.

We don't collect any royalties when companies buy applications on AppExchange, but as customers adopt additional applications running on our service, they will be much less likely to leave us for a competitor. With AppExchange, we evolved beyond being a technology provider to becoming an enabler of innovative technology. Much of our future rests on this developing ecosystem.

Without an ecosystem of partners to further a company's vision, even companies with extraordinary services can be relegated to being niche players. Opportunities to grow can become limited. Be open to partnering with others to expand your capabilities and service.

Think about what Apple did with the iPod; Apple has an entire ecosystem of companies that make speakers, headphones, and cases catering to that device. These accessories offer iPod users more ways to enjoy their device.

It's flattering when other companies build something to further develop or enhance your product or service, but don't accept everything that comes your way. The iPod ecosystem has been so successful because Apple carries only those products that meet its exacting standards. Apple users trust Apple-authorized dealers and continue to do so because the company has not made any compromises. It's imperative that you never do anything that might squander a customer's trust.

Play #61: Harness Customers' Ideas

We have been on a constant quest to grow our customer community, and we build offline and online forums to do so. In 2004, we launched a Web site for customers who successfully self-implemented our service, as a way for them to share their experiences with others using the service or with those considering it. Over time, we began to experiment with blogs, message boards, and other forms of social media. We had tens of thousands of customers giving advice—and we needed a way to take advantage of this phenomenon. Calling upon crowd sourcing models and Web sites like Digg, which allow users to share, discover, and vote on content, we created the ability for customers to vote on and rate ideas posted by the community.

This tool evolved into more than a souped-up suggestion box. We called it IdeaExchange, and it became the editorial board of the site. It also offered a way for us to introduce an idea and observe how it resonated with our community. Some ideas were validated, and we decided to invest in them. Others got weeded out before anyone wasted their time. The site became, as Jamie Grenney, our Ideas product manager, likes to call it, "a global focus group that never sleeps." Since we've launched it, we've received eleven thousand ideas, 257,000 votes, and twenty-six thousand comments—all written by customers. (It's also how we tested—and decided upon—a title for this book.)

Our developer partners have also found IdeaExchange to be a fertile ground. One start-up company, Appirio, had been thinking about building integration capabilities between Google and Salesforce. Then, Appirio cofounder Narinder Singh saw a post on IdeaExchange calling for a way to let information from

Salesforce accounts to appear on a Google home page. The post was actually written by Jamie, who runs IdeaExchange, and we all thought it was a good suggestion, but we didn't have time to build this additional functionality. Appirio did, and within six weeks it created it and launched it on AppExchange. It quickly became the top application.

This application was successful not just because Appirio is a partner that we like but because it built a compelling service for customers. Only the best applications—the ones customers like the most—bubble to the top. This system is completely different from the way the software industry (defined by companies and customers having an adversarial relationship) had operated for the past fifty years.

IdeaExchange became our secret weapon for innovation. One day, over e-mail, I mentioned the success we were having with this system to my friend Michael Dell. Michael had just taken back the reins as CEO of Dell, and he was looking for ways for the company to move faster and become more innovative. "Dell should have an ideas engine," I said. The system would provide a scalable way to collect and capture feedback from the Dell customer community.

Within three weeks, Dell launched IdeaStorm—built on the Salesforce Ideas platform—to give Dell customers and enthusiasts a chance to become a part of the product development process. IdeaStorm was an immediate success. The day the site launched, a user suggested that Dell sell computers with the Linux platform preinstalled. In the coming weeks, tens of thousands of users agreed, and the post ranked as the number-one idea for months. Three months later, as a direct result of this intelligence, Dell released several consumer notebooks and desktops with the Linux operating system preinstalled. Using the

Internet and our Ideas technology platform, Dell has gained the ability to listen to its customers. As Jeff Howe explains in his book, *Crowdsourcing: Why the Power of the Crowd Is Driving the Future of Business*, "Dell's IdeaStorm attempts to capture the collective intelligence of the crowd. . . . It's using the crowd to brainstorm new innovations."[2] The result? Ideas turning into revenue within months.

Michael Dell, pleased with the immediate return on investment, shared his experience with Howard Schultz of Starbucks. He even did a demo for him. (Michael makes one hell of a sales engineer.) Like Michael, Howard had recently reclaimed the CEO title of the company he had founded. Having grown from a single store to the largest coffeehouse company in the world, Starbucks was looking for a way to reconnect and reengage in a regular dialogue with its customers. Before I knew it, I was having lunch with this legendary entrepreneur to tell him about the tool we had developed. Thirty days later, we signed a deal with Starbucks, and the company soon launched MyStarbucksIdea.com. Howard soon revealed in a shareholders meeting that it was one of the company's five key initiatives and commented in *BusinessWeek* that the adoption of this tool would change his company and instill what he called "a seeing culture."[3]

This online community, which allows Starbucks customers to share ideas and to vote on them and discuss them, has in fact allowed the company to see what its customers want. As Chris Bruzzo, vice president of Starbucks brand and online marketing, puts it: this "is helping our customers shape the future at Starbucks." The company has received seventy thousand ideas and executed dozens of them that have improved its business and has used the community to report back on improvements, including free AT&T Wi-Fi access for iPhone users, a richer hot chocolate, and ready-brew instant coffee. One of their most unusual responses to customer feedback was debuting "splash sticks," which fit into the hole in the lid to prevent coffee from spilling while someone is walking or driving.

There is no doubt that managing the ideas of customers is making Starbucks more beloved by customers as well as more innovative. "I was floored. It was like Starbucks was reading my mind. That little stick made my whole morning," Angela Vargo wrote in a blog response to the initiative.

Becoming Part of Your Customer's Dialogue

In this new age of nonstop, immediate communication in blogs, wikis, Twitter, and YouTube, you can be fairly certain that your customers are having a very public conversation about your products and practices. Every company needs to find a way to become relevant in its customers' conversations. As Michael Dell said in *BusinessWeek*, "These conversations are going to occur whether you like it or not, O.K.? Well, do you want to be part of that or not? My argument is you absolutely do. You can learn from that. You can improve your reaction time. And you can be a better company by listening and being involved in that conversation."[4]

Right now, every business must determine:

- How can my business be a part of this conversation?
- How can my business learn from it?
- How can my business use it to innovate?

Play #62: Develop Communities of Collaboration (aka Love Everybody)

Early on, we recognized that we needed other companies, both big and small, to partner with us and develop online software that complemented our own. This is not a new idea, but traditional software companies like Siebel or SAP never truly empowered their partners. They never made a capital investment. We saw many smaller companies taking a bet on our service, and we decided that we should support them in order to truly benefit from the massive potential power of collaboration.

We wanted to be close to these companies and remove as much of the risk for their businesses as possible. Why not provide a self-contained environment where they could connect with the people who invented the industry? This was the impetus for the salesforce.com apps development incubator.

We leased a facility in San Mateo, California, and began renting cubicles to start-ups that wanted to build their businesses on top of our platform. (We charge a fee that allows us to break even, but we do not make a profit.) We provide on-site programmers to help with coding questions, we introduce start-ups to potential customers, and we help them market their services.

Companies were immediately drawn to the opportunity because it made sense. "I don't want to manage infrastructure," Narinder Singh, the cofounder of Appirio, explained. "We have a business to build, and I want to focus 100 percent on that." Narinder used to work on corporate strategy at SAP, and with his familiarity with its products and his connections to its executives, it would have made sense to launch a start-up that supported SAP. Narinder didn't even consider it. "The bet we had to make with SAP was so daunting. We weren't going to get the attention of SAP; it was a closed system, even if we were on the inside," Narinder said. Besides, "I worked with smart people, but if you're driving a go-cart, I don't care if Mario Andretti is at the wheel; you aren't going to win the race." Narinder believed in the revolution in the cloud, and we did everything we could to make it easier for him to join our force.

Providing developers with both a platform and a community (and a lot of free T-shirts) has generated a fleet of one hundred sixty thousand developers who are innovating more rapidly than ever before. Take, for example, the fact that AppExchange launched with seventy applications and by 2008 offered more than eight hundred applications. As *Wired* magazine stated, this new model is "delivering silicon power to the people."[5] This ability for anyone to use the Internet to create and sell applications is the next computing paradigm. Finally, The End of Software is here.

Play #63: Evolve by Intelligent Reaction

There's a lot of controversy when it comes to theories about evolution, but when it comes to evolution in the software industry, there's only one theory that makes sense: surviving by learning from experience and usage patterns. My friend Adam Bosworth, the Web and software pioneer, describes this organic learning process as "intelligent reaction."

A normal development cycle in the technology industry is three years. At salesforce.com, it's ninety days. We make minor upgrades every week and unveil a major release every three to four months. (We brand these according to the seasons, as the fashion industry does.) With this process, innovation is constant and our customers participate in the maturation process.

Constant releases ensure that we receive real-time feedback from the marketplace, which helps direct our next moves. Ultimately, it's far simpler to make adjustments to small steps than it is to fix huge leaps that fall flat in the marketplace. These small developments also play a big role in dictating product evolution.

Intelligent reaction—or going where our business takes us—is what has always dictated our next move and how we evolved from an application to a platform company. Salesforce.com could not have started as a platform. We needed a critical mass of end users, the hundreds of thousands of customers using the application and providing input so that we could see what they were looking for and know how to build additional functionality that suited them. It is the user community, or customer base, that ultimately gives a company "permission" (through their demands and, eventually, purchases) to launch new products and enter new markets.

There are new rules in business today. Users have more power than ever. That is not something you should fear. Successfully scaling a product and growing a company are much easier when you've engaged the end user as an active participant in the process.

PART 6

The Corporate Philanthropy Playbook
How to Make Your Company About More Than Just the Bottom Line

Play #64: The Business of Business Is More Than Business

We started salesforce.com with a goal to create a different type of company. Our vision was to build a different technology model (Software-as-a-Service), a different sales model (subscription based), and a different philanthropic model (integrated into the for-profit corporation from the very beginning). Each of these ideas emanated from our disenchantment with the traditional manner in which things were done. The philanthropic effort in particular, though, stemmed from a personal experience.

Early in my career, during my first few years at Oracle, I defined my success by making money and achieving power.

By my early thirties, however, I realized that these superficial achievements did not provide real meaning or true happiness. Despite a list of impressive titles and a pile of material possessions, I felt that something was missing, and began to consider my place in the world and how I could make a difference.

The opportunity to take a six-month sabbatical from Oracle and a trip to India spurred a profound change in me, but no one at Oracle understood what I had experienced or accepted my transformation. Larry Ellison expressed fatherly concern that I'd gone off the deep end, and Ray Lane, then Oracle's president, didn't appreciate my desire to talk about these ideas ("I didn't understand it. He was as likely to talk about getting in touch with yourself as he was to talk about [the specifics of] a product design," he later said about me.[1]) My colleague and friend Evan Goldberg lamented the loss of my happy-go-lucky days. In some ways I could appreciate the confusion, as everyone was accustomed to my collecting toys, driving fast cars, and otherwise living largely. Why would I suddenly embrace such dramatically different interests?

It was as if by divine intervention that shortly after I returned from my trip to India and my enlightening meeting with Ammachi, I was invited to attend the Presidents' Summit for America's Future. In 1997 General Colin Powell, who just had retired as chairman of the Joint Chiefs of Staff, and the five living presidents stood up together and launched America's Promise, a program that urged the nation to make a greater commitment to its youth.

I had never before been a part of a conversation that suggested businesses use all of their assets—their equity, their capital, their people, their relationships—to serve as a force for good in the world. This was different from what I had learned in school, and it challenged the accepted thinking of esteemed economists, such as Milton Friedman, who famously said, "The business of business is business." I was immediately attracted to this radical idea, and I felt compelled to participate.

I returned from the event and told Larry Ellison about the summit with great enthusiasm. He was immediately receptive and in fact revealed that he had been interested in launching a foundation at Oracle. The purpose was to outfit economically challenged public schools with networked computers. Larry wanted to commit $100 million from Oracle over ten years to create this program.

Fast-forward a few months, and suddenly I was in charge of the company's first major philanthropic initiative. It was with great fanfare that we launched Oracle's Promise, our own variant on the America's Promise initiative, at New York City's Radio City Music Hall in 1997. I had the opportunity to meet General Powell, who endorsed the cause and soon became a mentor. He gave me advice on how to take the lead in this effort and encouraged me to grant employees time off to volunteer.

It was exciting to oversee this program, but it was extraordinarily challenging as well. I didn't have any experience running a philanthropic initiative, and the nonprofit world was often dubious about the sincerity of a for-profit company's intentions, especially considering that Oracle had no track record in this area. At the same time, the opportunity introduced personal challenges. My responsibilities to develop and market new products at Oracle didn't wane. Half my time was spent in management meetings in glistening office towers in Redwood Shores, and the other half was spent in dilapidated schools in South Central Los Angeles; Washington, DC; Northern Ireland; and Israel.

Despite the challenges that came with blending these two roles, I found much of the work to be rewarding. On the surface, the program succeeded in its mission. We placed thousands of computers in hundreds of schools worldwide. We touched the lives of tens of thousands of young people. And, although this wasn't the impetus of the effort, Oracle reaped positive recognition that benefited the company. (Larry was even interviewed on the *Oprah Winfrey Show*.)

Ultimately, however, the program fell very short of its full potential—something that became evident during an embarrassing fiasco at the MacFarland Middle School in Washington, DC. Oracle had been tapped to wire this school as a special favor to General Powell. The school was spread out over several floors and terribly run down.

The temperature climbed to a scorching 110 degrees on the day of the installation, and the humidity was suffocating. The school didn't have any elevators, and there were only three people on our team to get the job done. No one came to volunteer from the school, and although local Oracle employees had previously committed to participating, they never arrived. It was close to the end of the quarter, which meant employees were busy selling and trying to make their numbers. No one viewed participating in the volunteer event with any seriousness. They certainly didn't think it would reflect negatively on them if they didn't show up. After all, wasn't a 100 percent focus on the bottom line the most important thing? In 1997, that was the belief that guided corporate America.

Still, it was an incredibly humbling experience to have to call General Powell and explain that we had failed to complete the task. I couldn't hear his response because we had a bad connection. That was probably for the best. I think he might have hung up on me.

About thirty minutes after the awful phone call, a battalion of U.S. Marines swept into the school. Our team was caught by surprise when they said they were there to install the computers. Although there was relief in knowing that this force would get the job done, it didn't give me much solace. Oracle had its own army of fifty thousand tech-savvy employees, several thousand of them just a few miles away; why did we require the Marines' assistance to set up computers in a middle school?

The experience forced me to consider the shortcomings of the program. I realized that although in theory doing good was a relatively short order for a corporation, it was too tall a task to simply tack on. I understood that to succeed, such a program had to be woven into the fabric of an organization.

I began to consider how to make a philanthropic program part of a company's DNA. I knew that if we had been able to draw on Oracle's full assets—its employees, customers, products, money, and partners—we could have made a much more substantial contribution. This idea became a passion of mine, and it further ignited my interest in starting my own company.

Play #65: Integrate Philanthropy from the Beginning

Parker, Dave, and Frank, the salesforce.com cofounders, were receptive to the idea of building a business that simultaneously gave back to the community. We all shared the philosophy that the value of a corporation should be distributed not only to its leadership but also to the communities in which it operates and to the world. We discussed these ideas on our first day of work, and filed the Salesforce Foundation as a 501(c)(3) public charity at the same time that we incorporated salesforce.com. The foundation was seeded with personal money, but the ultimate goal was for the company's equity and assets to sustain and grow it.

My experience with Oracle's Promise taught me that goodwill and sincere intentions were not enough to build a strong corporate foundation. It would require the leadership of someone with experience in both the nonprofit and corporate worlds. A friend recommended Suzanne DiBianca, a management consultant who did strategy and organization development with leaders of Fortune 500 companies. Prior to her corporate experience, Suzanne had served as a director of a nonprofit organization that works with NGOs and government officials to encourage peaceful resolution techniques for global and local conflict. I believed that this background had given her the skills necessary to bridge both the nonprofit and for-profit worlds.

Suzanne officially joined as the executive director of the Salesforce Foundation in 2000. Over the next few months, we researched established corporate foundations and personally met with dozens of foundation directors, including those at Cisco Systems, Hewlett-Packard, and Levi Strauss & Co. There was much to learn from the experiences of these companies, and it was our intention to unearth the best practices in corporate social responsibility.

Play #66: Make Your Foundation Part of Your Business Model

The insight we gained from other companies was tremendous. eBay, for example, had endowed its foundation with $1 million of corporate stock prior to the company's 1998 initial public offering. It was one of the pioneers in providing company equity to fund philanthropic goals, and we were captivated by the power of this model. As the company grew, the foundation grew proportionately. I knew that salesforce.com could be the energy to power the foundation; the founders agreed to place more than 1 percent of salesforce.com founding stock into the foundation, and we couldn't wait to see it take charge.

The commitment to set aside 1 percent of equity was the first step to building the 1-1-1 model that would eventually guide our foundation. The idea for the second 1 percent commitment—1 percent of employees' time—was inspired by the program at Hasbro, the creator of such toys as Mr. Potato Head and G.I. Joe. I had met Hasbro's chairman, Alan Hassenfeld, at the World Economic Forum in Davos, Switzerland. Hasbro was started by Alan's grandfather in the 1920s, and the company had embraced a tradition of philanthropy since its earliest days. Alan was extremely generous in sharing Hasbro's experience and serving as a mentor. "It's the job of the chairman or CEO to set the ethics of a company. If the leadership truly believes in what it is saying and acts accordingly, that emanates through the entire corporation," he said. I understood I would have to evangelize these values, but Alan told me that wouldn't be enough. "It's one thing to talk about it; it's another to try to get your people involved and empowered."

One of the ways Hasbro empowered its employees was by offering four hours a month of paid time off to perform community service. With that investment of time, Hasbro employees have made innumerable visits to seriously ill kids, built incredible playgrounds for children with disabilities, and participated in life-changing programs like Operation Smile. The people who worked at Hasbro knew they were contributing

The 1-1-1 Model

From its inception, the Salesforce Foundation used a unique model of integrated philanthropy, one designed to grow with the company. Our 1-1-1 model disseminates a portion of the financial and intellectual wealth of the organization to those most in need:

- **1 percent equity:** using 1 percent of founding stock to offer grants and monetary assistance to those in need, especially to support youth and technology programs

- **1 percent time:** finding meaningful activities for salesforce.com employees during their six paid days off a year devoted to volunteerism, and promoting a culture of caring

- **1 percent product:** facilitating the donation of salesforce.com subscriptions to nonprofits, helping them increase their operating effectiveness and focus more resources on their core mission

The 1-1-1 Model in Action

A terrific example of how our 1-1-1 model works is a San Francisco initiative called Project Homeless Connect, which brings a wide variety of social service providers — housing experts, doctors, job

something meaningful, which made them feel more invested in the company and inspired them to do their best. I thought that secondary gain further justified the hours our employees would be spending outside our office. Maybe the volunteer program would prevent them from feeling as rudderless as I had during my time at Oracle. Building on the 1 percent allocation of equity, we decided to give employees more than 1 percent of their time—six paid days off annually—to volunteer.

coaches, people to fit eyeglasses, dentists, the DMV—together under one roof for the day. The program has become one of the most successful initiatives for dealing with the homeless, and has now become a national model. Following is an example of what impact we can make with what we call a full package: people, technology, and money.

- **1 percent equity:** We have given Project Homeless Connect grants to buy everyday necessities for clients, such as toiletry kits, sweatshirts, and sleeping bags.

- **1 percent time:** Our company participates in Project Homeless Connect every month with more than a hundred employees. They do everything from outreach and recruiting (including finding and bringing the homeless to the Civic Center) to walking them around to different doctors or services. Our employees bring their families and friends to help out—something we encourage.

- **1 percent product:** Our employees built an application on the Force.com platform to input the homeless client data, and customized it to meet the needs of Project Homeless Connect.

There was another resource that several companies had committed to donating to charitable causes: a portion of profits. Levi Strauss & Co., Merck & Co., and Ben & Jerry's, for example, had earmarked a percentage of their earnings or profits to go into their corporate foundations. Following their lead, we made a commitment to give 1 percent of our profits to community groups. We were not profitable when we made that commitment, and would not be for some time. We understood that although we would not immediately see the cash for this commitment, we needed to take a long-term approach. This eventually led to a 1 percent product initiative (whereby we donate the salesforce.com service in lieu of profits)—a contribution that we've since realized can have a much greater impact on a nonprofit organization (by helping it scale) than a cash donation might have.

Play #67: Choose a Cause That Makes Sense and Get Experts on Board

Salesforce.com is a technology company founded on a belief in the Internet as a democratizing tool; therefore, it's logical that our foundation aims to provide access to technology to young people in underserved communities. In 1999, when we launched our company, the digital divide, or the gap between those with and those without access to computers and the Internet—and the imbalance that gap created—was a matter of concern. I was troubled about this disparity, and I also recognized that the true power of the Internet rested on its reach being extended to the masses.

In 1998, legislation called E-Rate was passed in an effort to spur the deployment of high-speed Internet access to schools in low-income areas. Although the legislation was a positive step in improving access to the Internet in schools, it did not have any jurisdiction over after-school programs. We found this to be an overlooked area in which we could invest to make a difference. Through our ongoing relationship with Colin Powell and America's Promise, we connected with PowerUP, a nonprofit organization launched to combat the digital divide. It was seeded with $10 million from the family foundation of AOL founder Steve Case, and it sought to leverage partnerships with public and private organizations. The goal was to promote youth development through technology and to enhance young people's lives in after-school settings by wiring existing community centers such as YMCAs and Boys & Girls Clubs. Technology companies like Hewlett-Packard, Gateway, and Cisco Systems, as well as nontechnology companies such as PowerBar, saw the benefits of this model for collaboration to solve a community need.

Being connected with PowerUP and other companies that supported it was a great way to make an impact. The effort also made us realize how much work there was to be done. We needed a team, not just one dedicated person, to build a strong foundation. Immediately, I thought we could use the assistance of Julie Trell, a teacher and technology expert whom I had met two years earlier when I was working on a project for Oracle's Promise in Israel.

Julie and I had been introduced through a mutual friend, and when I told her about what we were doing at Oracle, she replied, "You can't just give computers to schools—you have to train teachers and youth workers!" I knew then she was right, and I was grateful when she offered to spend the next month volunteering her time to help with the training. Later she assisted us when Oracle wired schools in Atlanta, and I never forgot her advice to me: "If you start a foundation that focuses on schools and technology, you have to hire a teacher," she said. "You shouldn't just be a company that gives out computers and money. You need someone who is familiar with working with kids and education—it gives credibility and makes a deeper impact."

I wanted to ensure that we would be much more than a company that gave away computers and money. I handed Julie's resume to Suzanne. "Here's your first employee," I said.

Play #68: Share the Model

We opened our first after-school technology center at the Embarcadero YMCA in summer 2000. It was incredible to have Colin Powell, the original inspiration for this effort, in attendance. I had the opportunity to speak at the launch, which gave me the chance to share our model and enlist others to join our crusade. I was amazed by the potential of others joining and the possibility of encouraging this on a massive scale. What would happen, for example, if a top-tier venture capital firm required its portfolio companies to place 1 percent of their equity into a foundation serving the communities in which they did business? It was phenomenal to consider the good that we could generate and the positive impact it would have on society. We wouldn't need to depend on the generous gifts of wealthy donors. I wanted to evangelize this idea because I knew that our efforts—the contributions of one small start-up company—could only scratch the surface. "I challenge other Internet companies to follow suit and set aside a portion of their company stock toward community initiatives," I said to the attendees. "Those who aren't ready to start their own foundation are welcome to leverage our resources and infrastructure and join forces with our foundation by donating stock and volunteering time."

This was the beginning of an effort we would later develop into an initiative we called the Power of Us—and a cornerstone of our mission. By including our vendors and partners, we have been able to magnify our impact as well as strengthen relationships. Do not limit your philanthropic efforts to your company; you will be far more successful if you leverage your entire network.

The Case for Corporate Philanthropy

We believe that all businesses can and should help make the world a better place. We also believe there are rich rewards in doing so. Building partnerships between private enterprise and public interest produces profitable outcomes for everyone. Here are the top reasons why you should get started right away:

It's the Right Thing to Do (for the community and the company)

Empowering your communities stimulates business development and improves the bottom line. Better education translates into a more skilled workforce. Reduced poverty levels result in higher consumption.

It Builds Your Brand

Customers with a favorable impression of a company's philanthropy are three times more likely to be loyal customers than those who have less favorable perceptions about a company's philanthropic efforts.*

It Attracts and Retains Employees — Sparking a Competitive Advantage

Nearly two-thirds of Gen Y employees say they prefer to work for a company that provides opportunities for them to apply their skills to benefit nonprofit organizations.**

All things being equal, employees who have a favorable impression of their company's philanthropy are five times more likely to remain with their employer.*

It's Fun — Honest

It is a great way to get to know the people you work with (both employees and business partners), and it's rewarding to see that you can make an immediate impact.

*Council on Foundations and Walker Information, "National Benchmark Study: Measuring the Business Value of Corporate Philanthropy," May 2002.
**2007 Deloitte Volunteer IMPACT Survey

Play #69: Build a Great Program by Listening to the Constituents

The first salesforce.com-sponsored technology centers aimed at bridging the digital divide were a great idea in theory, and the centers were welcome additions to communities, but the program was fraught with serious challenges. PowerUP operated as a large-scale national program with a centralized approach. We found that the one-size-fits-all model didn't work at every center, and some centers were duplicating existing resources and services. Furthermore, although the program was effective in its mission of spreading computers across the land, it didn't dictate a coherent curriculum that communicated how to use or maintain the equipment. That, we soon found, was a big problem.

Salesforce.com employees rallied behind the effort right away, but the centers did not gain the traction we had anticipated. The students who attended weren't using computers for the first time; in fact, some of them knew more than many of the teachers. They weren't interested in playing games or learning the basics, but their teachers had little else to offer them. We realized that if we didn't give the students some relevant content quickly, we'd lose their interest—and our audience. The donated computer systems were on their way to becoming ridiculously expensive paperweights. We needed to immediately determine how to leverage our investment into something with real value to the people we wanted to serve.

Although computer-savvy students weren't the audience we had expected, we realized we still had an opportunity to make a contribution. We wouldn't be the first to introduce underserved youth in San Francisco to technology, but we could offer them a way to pursue their passion. Maybe this outcome would be even better than what we had anticipated. The kids who came to our centers were crazy about trying the latest machines and programs. In many ways they reminded me of myself when I was in school and played on the computers at RadioShack. That opportunity fueled my interest in technology—and gave me the confidence and inspiration to start my first business.

Steve Wright, a former Peace Corps volunteer, technologist, and high school educator working at the Beacon Initiative, which ran eight of the computer labs we supported, joined the foundation and helped us cater the program to our audience. Steve observed the students at work and discovered they were interested in exploring the Web, watching videos, listening to and making rap music, and trying to build pages online. They were drawn to interactive technology. (That was something we could appreciate!) Steve showed them how to make beats online and worked with Julie to teach filming and editing skills to help them produce their own films.

These young people had a lot to say about hard-hitting topics, including juvenile justice, gun violence, and homelessness, and our new focus on youth media took off. Our salesforce.com

BEHIND THE CLOUD

people loved it because it tapped their innate skills; the young people loved it because it gave them an effective, accepted, and creative way to share their ideas. The program taught technology skills that could help them stand out in school and the job market, and the experience fostered important interviewing and cooperation skills. I also appreciated that the program had measurable results. The participants' hard work resulted in film shorts and Web sites that the students took pride in showing.

In an effort to showcase the students' work, we hosted a Youth Media Festival. The first festival drew a crowd of more than three hundred, and the audience was surprised and impressed by the quality of the work. One of the films, a thirty-minute documentary called *Bus 24: The Diversity Bus* shared the experiences of young filmmakers ages ten to sixteen years old as they journeyed on the San Francisco Municipal Railway Bus 24 from the rougher edges of Bayview–Hunters Point to the more privileged parts of Pacific Heights. Many of these students had never left their own communities or experienced the way other people lived in less violent neighborhoods. The film captured the interactions they had with fellow riders, revealed the diversity of the city each of us called home—and gave all of us some hope.

As we expanded the foundation internationally (international offices have their own dedicated foundation staff once they grow to a certain capacity, usually seventy-five or more employees), the program evolved into an international media festival. We hosted events in San Francisco and London and flew our young filmmakers in from all over the world to present their work. As we witnessed how these films resonated with audiences, I decided it would be remarkable to bring some of these films and several young filmmakers to the World Economic Forum.

The students were excited to show their films at the conference in Davos, Switzerland, and they took their role as change agents very seriously. We spent months preparing and produced six films in three categories—health, poverty, and the Middle East. We invited young filmmakers, including Dannie, a sixteen-year-old from the United Kingdom; Ahmed, an eighteen-year-old from Bahariya Oasis, Egypt; and Dima, a fourteen-year-old from Sderot, Israel, to show their films and talk about their inspiration and the change they were trying to effect.

We had expected to garner attention, but we were shocked when the event drew an enormous crowd, including such prominent leaders as environmental activist and former U.S. vice president Al Gore, tech legend Michael Dell, and musician and human rights advocate Peter Gabriel. Some people had warned me that I was taking a big risk—after all, I was showing a room full of luminaries youth-made films, including one about teenagers and sexually transmitted diseases. I believed, however, that the audience at Davos would be receptive. People who are dedicated to making a difference in this world want to hear a young person's perspective. Although I didn't think it was a risk, I underestimated how pivotal it would be for these young people to share their films.

Dannie, who contributed a harrowing—but ultimately uplifting and hopeful—music video about self-harm, spoke passionately about why she and her friends made the film, their personal struggles, and how they've since committed to campaign on the issue of self-harm in schools. Theo, a San

Francisco student who has worked with the foundation practically since its inception, contributed a powerful film about homelessness in San Francisco. The city's mayor, Gavin Newsom, who attended the event, took the opportunity to speak about the ways his administration was trying to address the problems Theo raised in his film. Ahmed and Dima, who hailed from countries with a long and bitter rivalry, and couldn't communicate with one another in their native languages, discussed the unique opportunity to get to know one another.

"I like him," said Dima.

"He's my brother," replied Ahmed.

As the session closed, I realized that the biggest risk we took was not in inviting these young people to share their voices; the biggest risk would be ignoring what they had to say. It was obvious that the wisdom these young people offered outshined what we gave them. The students realized the power of their voices as well. The next day, Ahmed said, "What happened last night changed everything in my mind. When I saw the important people watch the film, I realized I have made something bigger. I am happy to see this. I didn't ever believe it would be like this. It was never in my dreams."

I was amazed by what we could achieve by giving young people opportunity and encouragement. Theo's film on homelessness in San Francisco helped build much needed awareness. Dannie's film about self-harm encouraged the United Kingdom's Parliament to increase the amount of money distributed to schools to fund a part-time counselor to help young people deal with emotional issues. The impact was real. Our mission to give people the tools and the platform to make a positive difference grew from there.

Play #70: Create a Self-Sustaining Model

In summer 2004, we witnessed the true financial power of our integrated model. Salesforce.com went public and became listed on the New York Stock Exchange. The initial public offering raised more than $12 million for the foundation in one day.

This event proved the capability of pre-IPO companies to make a positive difference through an early financial commitment of equity. The infusion of capital bolstered our foundation's ability to be self-sustaining and provided the opportunity to make bigger financial contributions to our communities. Prior to the IPO, the foundation was largely funded by private investments in the early days, but we needed cash to scale and grow. The IPO generated those funds and allowed us to develop a grants program to fund youth development and educational organizations. We also gained the financial freedom to embark on other innovative efforts.

One program was BizAcademy, a four-day entrepreneurial workshop designed for high school students in underserved school districts. The program was jointly developed with BizWorld, originally founded in 1993 by prominent venture capitalist Tim Draper. The idea for the BizWorld elementary school program was sparked when Tim's daughter asked him what he did all day at work. In an effort to explain business to his eight-year-old, he tapped his daughter's passion for making friendship bracelets and created an activity to teach young people about running their own businesses selling their creations. We appreciated the benefits of the program and tailored a version for high school students that fit with our company and incorporated our CRM technology. We called on the business talents of our salesforce.com team, venture capitalists, and other professionals around the world to teach the students how to become entrepreneurs. The program is hosted in our office, and the students are required to interact and network with our corporate employees, who are very different from them.

The goal is for the students to experience the ins and outs of running a company, and one of the most motivating factors is that they keep the profits they earn. Participants collaborate to manage all aspects of their business, from raising money and learning about finances, to manufacturing a product of their own creation (picture frames, clocks, potted plants), to marketing and selling their product using the salesforce.com application. Our third year into sponsoring the program, we changed the focus from selling a product to selling a service—something that dovetailed nicely with our business model. The students were charged with selling "green consulting" services, and they were responsible for researching, analyzing, and offering suggestions on how to solve each of salesforce.com departments' environmental challenges.

It's been incredible to witness how the students run their own businesses. During one of the recent programs, something extraordinary happened. The businesses were selling decorated potted plants, and although all the potted plants looked handmade and fairly similar, one of the teams decided to sell them at $25 apiece—about $10 more than the other teams. We didn't want to discourage them, but we suggested they consider lowering the price because their competitors' very similar product was priced so much lower. Samuel, the company president, was adamant about not wanting to change the price. He said that based on the demographics and salary ranges of the potential customers in the building, the price was something his target audience could afford. We didn't push it, and they went to market. Part of the marketing plan, the company then revealed, was to give a percentage of its profits to the environmental organization NativeEnergy. The result: it not only sold its products for significantly more than any of the other companies but also sold out faster, serving as an interesting case study for all of us.

We enjoy sponsoring this program and love the energy these young people bring into our office. Although it's undeniably fun, we take the program very seriously, and we expect the students to operate on a true professional business level. Students are matched with employees who help them build professional and social relationships and assist with schoolwork and college applications. The result of having such high expectations of the mentees has been astounding. The students gain business and technology skills as well as tremendous confidence.

There is a measurable goal to the program as well in helping the students win coveted internships, positions that are notoriously difficult for these teens to secure in their local communities. We teach them how to sell themselves by writing resumes, perfecting their pitch, networking, negotiating, and practicing interviews. More than 50 percent of the participants are matched with internships at local businesses. On average, about thirty interns work in salesforce.com offices around the globe each summer. BizAcademy is the vehicle we use to hire all our high school–age interns, and many stay with us well into their college careers. For example, Cristina Lam, one of our first BizAcademy graduates, now works for the foundation as a community involvement coordinator. Jessica Huang, who's been with our professional services department since 2006, has been so valuable that we created a way for her to work year round while attending school.

We've hosted fifteen academies around the world, and our first class of graduates is now halfway through college. Many, including Cristina, are on college scholarships provided by the foundation. In other instances, graduating from the program has been a springboard for a permanent job. Take Edmond Asante, a participant in our UK program, whom we met through one of our nonprofit partners, Landmark Training, which works with young people who have left school. We collaborated with Landmark on a BizAcademy program to introduce young people to the possibility of looking for employment beyond their immediate neighborhood supermarkets and stores. Edmond was hired as a trainee at HBV Enterprise, a consultancy in London that helps entrepreneurs start and grow their businesses. He gained confidence and excelled at HBV, and before long, he was offered a full-time salaried job.

Play #71: Share Your Most Valuable Resources—Your Product and Your People

The decision to give 1 percent of our profits in the form of product donation wasn't our idea. It came directly from requests from nonprofits. Less than six months after we officially launched our company, we got a call from a group of students at *Business Today*, the largest student-run magazine in the nation. The nonprofit, originally started in 1968 by three Princeton undergrads (including Steve Forbes) and run each year by a new team of graduating seniors, asked us for a free subscription to salesforce.com. They were in search of a way to manage their data amid the constant management changes, and thought salesforce.com might be the answer.

Around the same time, an employee in marketing came to us and requested a salesforce.com subscription for Rainforest2Reef, a conservation group that protects part of Mexico's 1.8-million-acre Calakmul Biosphere Reserve from deforestation. The employee had been volunteering at the nonprofit and believed that our service could help it manage its pipeline and communicate with its members more efficiently. We donated our service to help the organization automatically update its records and track how people find it. This resulted in immediate increased traffic. "What we used to get in one month, we now might see in one day," says Cheri Sugal, Rainforest2Reef's executive director.

As the salesforce.com application became more sophisticated and more customizable, its relevance to nonprofits grew exponentially. We know that introducing these groups to a technology that is easy to use can dramatically improve how they manage their information and can make a difference to the bottom line. (Rainforest2Reef has seen a fivefold revenue increase by using the service!)

We formally began our 1 percent product donation program by giving subscriptions of the service to organizations that we already supported financially, such as WITNESS, a nonprofit that uses video and online technologies to expose human rights violations. We searched for other nonprofits interested in using cutting-edge technologies to better manage their organizations. Many approached us for subscriptions as well. By 2008, more than five thousand nonprofits across fifty-two countries, including the Red Cross, Stanford University, United Way, Teach First, Microloan Foundation, and Ashoka, were using the donated application and operating more efficiently.

It's been amazing to see what these organizations have been able to achieve with the salesforce.com platform. The Children's Aid Society Carrera Adolescent Pregnancy Prevention Program, which educates teens about the consequences of sexual activity, was able to convert from a paper-based environment to an electronic one through salesforce.com, which reduced turnaround times, improved data integrity, and helped save countless trees. The Google Foundation has used the application to track every facet of its work, including the distribution of more than $150 million in grants to organizations that are addressing the world's most pressing problems.

The UN World Food Programme, the international community's frontline agency in fighting hunger, used the service to improve the management of donor relations activities and streamline fundraising operations—enabling it to raise funds significantly faster and allowing the organization's officers to save time. "Our donor relations officers need to focus their time and attention on activities that directly raise funds for the poor," Corinne Fleischer, the chief of donor relations for the UN World Food Programme in Asia, told us. "Put simply, the more time we focus on new partnerships, the more people we can feed."

Anyone Can Start an In-Kind Product Donation Program

One way to get your philanthropic programs started easily is to begin by providing your product or service for free or at a dramatically discounted rate to nonprofits. Gather a team of people to think creatively about how your product or service might help answer a social problem or move a nonprofit's mission forward.

Play #72: Involve Your Partners, Your Vendors, Your Network

Our partners, experts in building and deploying new technologies, witnessed how we were leveraging our resources for the community, and began asking us how they could get involved. In 2002, Eric Berridge, the cofounder of Bluewolf Group, an on-demand software consultancy, called us for advice about building a corporate philanthropic program. At first the company participated in volunteer events we had planned, such as delivering turkeys to soup kitchens during the holidays or working in a shelter for women who were the victims of domestic violence. By joining forces, we were able to accomplish more. There was another benefit in that we got to know one another—something that helped us collaborate better as business partners.

Bluewolf eventually established its own 1-1-1 model. It's become an important part of the company, and, like us, Bluewolf uses its foundation as a recruiting tool. "It attracts the right kind of people," Eric says. "Someone who donates their time has to be willing to go above and beyond the call of duty—and these are the types of people who build up an entrepreneurial culture."

Bluewolf's two hundred employees give back in a variety of ways, from helping senior citizens write their resumes to tutoring high school students. As at salesforce.com, the Bluewolf staff drives the program. It was the employees' idea to establish a scholarship fund that allows two students every year to attend university and study technology. Bluewolf has seen benefits to its business, too. As a consulting company, it sells its skills at integrating salesforce.com into different types of companies. It uses its pro bono experience of rolling out salesforce.com at thirty New York City schools (to help them track attendance, test scores, and disciplinary actions) as a calling card. "I can take that story to any company," Eric says. "They know if we did that successfully, we can do anything."

It's obvious that we amplify the difference we are trying to make if we include business partners like Bluewolf. Tapping the power of collaboration and leverage, we made this a formal pursuit with the Power of Us, a program that invites our partners to provide donated or discounted services or to develop new functionality for the nonprofit sector. The goal is to make it easy for them to get involved and for us to harness the potential power of our entire ecosystem.

It's working. CRM Fusion, for example, built an application that allows salesforce.com to work with PayPal, which allowed organizations like Rainforest2Reef to receive donations automatically—eliminating the need to pay anyone to input any data manually. Theikos (now part of Astadia), one of salesforce.com's implementation partners, got the system for the UN World Food Programme up and running, customized, and ready to service its operations across Asia in less than five weeks. Another salesforce.com partner, Swift River Consulting, created custom objects in salesforce.com for Wardrobe for Opportunity, an organization that provides free interview and working wardrobes to low-income job seekers, so that it could track the number of clients it served as well as manage the work of its volunteers.

One of the best parts of my job has been introducing this concept to diverse audiences. A number of years ago, I was speaking about our programs at a Stanford lecture hall where two young entrepreneurs, Larry Page and Sergey Brin, were sitting in the first row. "We are starting a company named Google that will do no evil," they said. (I had never heard of it.) "We want to do this." And they did. "Google.org was thrilled to copy, emulate, and 'steal' the wonderful salesforce.com model of 1 percent equity and 1 percent profit," says Dr. Larry Brilliant, the former executive director of Google.org and the president of The Skoll Foundation's Urgent Threats Fund. "Marc Benioff is a visionary, and Larry and Sergey have continually acknowledged him as the inspiration for their plan for Google's philanthropy."

This might be our greatest contribution. Google.org is now worth more than $2 billion and is making a real difference in addressing some of the world's most urgent problems. We are equally proud of inspiring other companies, including NetSuite, iRobot, LiveOps, and PalmOne, which are further developing a similar model. Collaboration and leverage have proven the Power of Us.

Play #73: Let Employees Inspire the Foundation

From the foundation's earliest days—actually from the time it was just a seedling of an idea—we determined that for it to be successful, it had to be driven by the interests of our employees. Building a foundation that reflected their passions was the only way they would truly embrace it as theirs. There are many examples that demonstrate that they have. Take, for instance, what happened a few years ago when I opened our annual company-wide meeting for questions and Sue Amar, a premier support analyst, stood up and asked, "What are we doing about the environment?"

It was a good question, and I knew the answer, but instead of giving her some half-baked information on our recycling programs and initiatives we were considering, I decided to encourage her to contribute her ideas. "I'm not sure," I said. "You have six paid days to figure it out; I'll support you." I suggested that Sue speak with Suzanne, the foundation's executive director.

Not long after the meeting, Sue came back to me with a plan for saleforce.com to reduce its carbon footprint. These discussions began to take place around the time of the release of *An Inconvenient Truth,* the eye-opening film that captures Al Gore's crusade to halt global warming. Many people in our company rallied behind the cause.

Although we were energized about the effort, we were hardly experts in this area. We searched for leaders in this field and engaged respected organizations, including Clean Air-Cool Planet, NativeEnergy, and Conservation International, for guidance. With these partners' help, we found a way to neutralize the existing effect of our greenhouse gas emissions from our offices, data centers, and travel activity through investing in renewable energy projects. These investments helped finance the construction of several specific projects, such as a wind farm run by the Rosebud Sioux Tribe in South Dakota, a family dairy farm methane energy project, and an international carbon sequestration project in the Makira forest of Madagascar.

This was a first step in becoming environmentally responsible. There are additional investments we've made—much closer to home—that are just as important. We've developed local programs to support recycling and composting, and an effort to assess office equipment, including looking at ways to reduce paper waste. We've also begun to subsidize commuter travel, and created incentives such as a Bike to Work grant, in which we donate a dollar to a local nonprofit organization for every mile biked.

In addition, we established the Earth Council, an entirely volunteer-run group that examines grassroots changes that can be made within the company to help thwart the climate crisis. It likely comes as no surprise that the leader of the Earth Council during its first year was Sue Amar. Later, as we expanded our effort, we assigned Sue to a new role as the first sustainability manager at salesforce.com, tasked with helping our company establish an environmental mission statement and working to integrate policies that support sustainable business practices.

This is not the only example of our employees taking initiative and ownership of the company's efforts to make a difference. In late August 2005, Hurricane Katrina, one of the deadliest hurricanes in U.S. history, devastated much of the north central Gulf Coast. Considering that we are a technology company based in San Francisco, it seemed that our biggest contribution to relief efforts would be financial. In fact, we raised more than $1 million, but that's not all that happened.

Within twenty-four hours of the levee breaking in New Orleans, seventy employees gathered on an impromptu conference call to discuss ways to combine the different Katrina survivor lists and share vital information. They built a searchable database called the PeopleFinder project, purchased the URL katrinalist.net, and created a Web site that accessed the database. The salesforce.com employees conceived of the project on Friday, September 2, and the initial data entry was completed with more than ninety thousand entries by Tuesday, September 7. They collaborated with other foundations to build and deploy the technology, and ultimately dozens of technologists and thousands of volunteers on the Internet helped make it happen. The list eventually grew to more than 650,000 entries, and has served millions of searches.

Our three thousand employees have donated more than one hundred fifty thousand hours to the communities that we serve. Of our global workforce, 85 percent is active in volunteering. (The national average of individuals who volunteer is 26 percent, according to the Bureau of Labor Statistics of the U.S. Department of Labor.)

These people—people who are inspired to create change, people who are confident that the work they do matters, people who are dedicated to something bigger than themselves—are the best employees in the world. These are the people every company should vie to hire and work to retain. These are the people who always go a step beyond and whose work builds an exceptional company.

How to Build an Employee-Inspired Foundation

Start from the Very Beginning
All new hires at salesforce.com learn about the foundation — and participate in a volunteer activity — during their new-hire orientation.

Canvass Employees About Their Interests
We ask employees what they want to focus on, which generates a sense of ownership.

Establish a Formal Structure to Elicit Employee Involvement
We set up employee-led foundation councils to serve as independent advisory groups of salesforce.com employees to the foundation for

each of our 1 percents — product, time, equity — as well as our One with the Earth effort.

Make the Foundation Part of Your Company by Making It Visible

At salesforce.com, foundation employees sit with company employees. Most of our company meetings include reports on our community service projects.

Recognize the Efforts of Employees

Every year, we honor a few exceptional people in each region who have gone above and beyond the call of duty. Each Volunteer of the Year recipient is awarded a grant of $500 in the winner's name made to an organization of his or her choice. We also send thank-you e-mails to volunteers — and copy their managers — after we receive feedback from nonprofit organizations about the difference these volunteers have made.

Foster the Foundation in Good Times and Bad

It's difficult to continue to invest in the foundation in dark times, but it's necessary. One time we held a volunteering event on a day when we were forced to have some layoffs. There was discussion as to whether or not we should cancel the event. "No, people need this more than ever," I said. "This keeps people connected to us." Canceling would have sent the wrong message. We were not going to turn our back on the community when times were tough.

Let It Evolve and Change

Embrace dynamism in everything you do!

Note: For everything you'll need, from advice on structuring a program to securing board alignment and resources, such as job descriptions and sample equity documents, please see www.sharethemodel.org.

Play #74: Have Your Foundation Mimic Your Business

In areas all over the globe, the salesforce.com application and platform have affected how nonprofits, including Habitat for Humanity and Susan G. Komen for the Cure, run their organizations. The demand for the service has also led to a new business initiative at salesforce.com and a new opportunity for the foundation. Our 1 percent product contribution specified that we give nonprofits ten subscriptions for free and offer any additionally requested subscriptions at an 80 percent discount. There were many nonprofit organizations, such as Stanford, that were using the service and unaware of the discount.

In an effort to build awareness around this program, we created a group within the company to focus exclusively on higher education and large NGO accounts that needed more than ten donated subscriptions. Although these organizations were paying a deeply discounted rate for the service (80 to 90 percent of the list price), the sheer number of paying customers and users created significant revenue. On average, the total amount of revenue from higher education and large NGOs amounted to approximately $2 million a year.

We decided to do something radical: shift the group that focused on higher education and large NGOs—and the revenue they generated—from the corporation to the foundation. This change offered an incredible opportunity to ensure the foundation's sustainability and expansion.

Most foundations do not operate this way; instead of building (non-fundraising-related) programs that generate revenue, they determine that they can spend only a certain percentage of the endowment (usually 5 percent) annually. Although that makes sense as a way to sustain the endowment, it limits the types of projects a foundation can afford to fund, and limits growth. By instituting an annual spending cap, we determined that our endowment could last fifteen to twenty years—but it would not guarantee perpetuity.

Innovative nonprofits have historically achieved true sustainability by embracing a revenue-generating business model. Since 1917, the Girl Scouts organization has held an annual cookie sale, which uses the nonprofit's resources—an army of enterprising young people—to sell cookies. The organization has further extended its reach by partnering with such companies as Nestlé, which churns Samoas, Tagalongs, and Thin Mint cookies into its Edy's ice cream and directs a portion of the proceeds to the Girl Scouts. Another example is the National Geographic Society, an organization founded more than 120 years ago to educate people about the world. The Society collected membership dues and launched the magazine as a giveaway to members to spur enrollment. Later, National Geographic supplemented that revenue stream with its cable network, films, and DVDs, making it the largest nonprofit scientific and educational institution in the world and a billion-dollar business! By blurring the lines between nonprofit and for-profit models as these organizations have, our foundation will increase its ability to sustain itself—and make a greater impact.

The foundation has grown in tandem with our company. One of our most exciting achievements was reaching one million subscribers—a milestone for our company and the SaaS industry. To celebrate, we donated a total of $1 million to ten nonprofit organizations.

Since inception we've given away $14 million in grants to deserving nonprofits, but we have gained much more. The foundation has made us a better company. It has served as a tool for collaboration with other companies. It has made our employees more fulfilled, more productive, and more loyal. It has made all of us happier. I did not know this would be the case, but our customers also have greater appreciation for us because of our philanthropic work. Customers have rallied behind our cause, arriving at our conferences early to help build playgrounds and paint schools (even in the rain). This is not why we do it, but the opportunity to work on something bigger together has positively affected our bottom line.

When I reflect on the past ten years, I see that our greatest contribution has been in creating a population of change agents. I'm proud of our employees, who have broadened their lives and the lives of young people, from at-risk students in San Francisco to young girls in Africa. We've been excited to have our partners join our forces and see employees go off on their own and take what they've learned at salesforce.com with them. This is a way we've found to create a legacy.

PART 7

The Global Playbook
How to Launch Your Product and Introduce Your Model to New Markets

Play #75: Build Global Capabilities into Your Product

Very few companies launch with the mandate to go global from the beginning. The general belief is that in order to prosper internationally, a start-up must first establish a rock-solid commercial base at home.

Although I did not want to act hastily, I was not willing to wait for long to grow salesforce.com beyond its Silicon Valley roots. The need for CRM is universal, so I thought we would be successful everywhere. International companies desperately needed our service, as did geographically scattered organizations that had to function as a single, cohesive unit. My perspective toward overseas expansion was that there was little time to waste.

We had considered the international potential of our service from the very earliest days of our company. We had built the Salesforce application so that the user could configure it to any currency and almost any language (even character-based languages) with just the click of a button. This on-the-fly translation feature was included in the earliest release, and although it was radical at the time, we never charged anything extra for it. This idea stemmed from my work at Oracle with principal technologist Yoshi Oikawa; it demonstrated that global capabilities were not an add-on feature but an intrinsic part of our service.

Remember, though, that simply having a Web site in another language doesn't mean you have a presence in that market. Translation must permeate throughout the whole organization: several clicks down on the Web site, in the help text, and with the people answering the phones. Also don't forget to rely on local experts for assistance with idiomatic and colloquial translation. Reportedly, when KFC entered China, its advertising slogan "finger-lickin' good" was mistranslated into Chinese characters that meant "eat your fingers off." Work with both experts and customers to ensure that all translation makes sense.

Play #76: Inject Local Leaders with Your Corporate DNA

Our international foray began in February 2000 when Fergus Gloster, David Dempsey, and John Appleby, executives who were running Oracle in Ireland, read a *BusinessWeek* article about salesforce.com and e-mailed me: "What are you doing about Europe?"

I was already focused on building an international presence, and it helped that now an opportunity presented itself in the form of a team that I trusted. I had previously collaborated with these executives on a philanthropic program in Belfast. After months of discussions about building the European market, we hired this team and brought them to San Francisco to meet everyone and really experience salesforce.com. We had outgrown our space in the Rincon Center, but our new offices weren't ready yet. In the meantime, our sales team had set up shop in a basement office. It wasn't ideal—there was a dreadful smell of garbage and a bad mouse problem. (Real estate in San Francisco had become so scarce that we were left with no other option.) Unfortunately, it was an especially malodorous garbage day when the European team came to visit.

The Irish executives came to our office wearing suits, but the rest of us were in our usual uniform of Hawaiian shirts, shorts, and baseball caps. Fergus seemed shocked by our informal attire and the NO SOFTWARE doormat adorned with dolphins. He was equally unnerved by the fact that I was training Koa, who was just a puppy, and had installed a fire hydrant in my office for this purpose. Koa used it successfully for the first time during the visit. I was so excited about Koa's success that the meeting broke up temporarily. "Oh my goodness, what have we gotten ourselves into? This is too California-esque," Fergus complained.

I figured that Fergus would recover from this culture shock quickly enough. Besides, we did pretty much everything differently at salesforce.com, so this served as a good introduction to the way our business worked. I couldn't wait to see what new ideas they would take back to Europe.

Play #77: Choose Your Headquarters and Territories Wisely

Although dogs and dolphins never made it to the office in Dublin, our approach to building our company in Europe wasn't that different from the approach to building it in the United States. We centered our sales operations with a corporate sales team (what other people call telesales) in one city to leverage training opportunities and build critical mass, just as we had done in the United States. At the time, Dublin was a prime place to establish our headquarters. The English-speaking city gave us a foot into the European market, and the corporate tax rate of 12.5 percent made it additionally appealing. We were hardly the first U.S. company to find Dublin compelling; Oracle, Microsoft, PayPal, and eBay also rooted themselves in Ireland for these reasons.

We rented a small office and began to build a talented corporate sales team by recruiting experienced people from Oracle, Dell, and other great companies. (We pledged to build a field sales team once corporate sales gained initial revenue and market share, just as we did in the United States.) The team was made up of native speakers: when a German customer called, he thought he was speaking to someone in Frankfurt; when a French customer called, she believed she rang someone in Paris. (We ensured that callers got to the right employee by having them call into local phone numbers, which were routed to our central phone bank. We also used e-mail and online forms to capture leads and then responded to these online inquiries in the language of the inquirer.)

This system went against the current model of selling enterprise software in Europe. At the time, it was believed that a CRM company would never be able to build business in such countries as France, Spain, or Sweden selling over the phone. The traditional model was to build a presence via a network of partnerships. It was the partners, operating in different countries, who did the groundwork to win customers and market share.

That strategy has merit inasmuch as partners can leverage local relationships and the partnership structure can help insulate a company against cash issues and foreign exchange rates. But it wouldn't work for us. Partners are paid on margin, which keeps the prices high for customers. That went against everything in our model. Besides, we really had no choice. When we started, there was no established European partner network that focused on on-demand, SaaS, or cloud computing solutions.

Our biggest challenge in Europe wasn't our unconventional selling strategy that initially relied on selling over the phone, but the fact that the on-demand message was still radically new. Once again, we had to educate the market about the model and create an industry. Businesses in the United Kingdom were just beginning to be introduced to concepts we had discussed domestically some eighteen months before. France was two to three years behind in terms of awareness.

The good news was that Europe was receptive to our message. The market loved the David versus Goliath strategy, and we launched the business in Europe by using the same tactics that dictated our strategies in the United States: free trials, building relationships with members of the press, and encouraging customer evangelism.

Think Like a Start-Up

A good guideline for global strategy is to think about the early start-up days. Recall how you got your first customers and how you tackled early challenges. Even consider using the original messaging — not the current messaging. You can't march into a new country and simply replicate what you are currently doing at home. It's possible that the new market isn't mature enough yet.

One of my mentors in global business, Chikara Sano, the former CEO of Oracle Japan, demonstrated the power of this idea when he committed to focusing Oracle Japan exclusively on becoming number one in database management. The company had already achieved that dominance in the United States and had evolved to build new applications and a consulting business. Although there was pressure to attempt to introduce these lines of business in Japan too, Sano-san stuck to what Oracle did when it first started, and ultimately built a very successful business in Japan.

In thinking like a start-up, abide by these three rules to help save infrastructure costs:

1. Translate the product on day one to the major languages, but only add additional languages as customer demand builds. (In Europe we've found merit to the "80-20 rule," whereby 80 percent of the revenue comes from 20 percent of the languages spoken in the region. Although we considered starting operations all over, we boiled it down to the United Kingdom, Germany, France, Spain, and the Nordic countries — and kept our focus there.)

2. Build a bedrock of small customers in each country before hiring local employees. This proves that the market is ready and the commitment is worth it.

3. Don't overhire. Employment laws overseas are complicated and largely favor the employee. When hiring sales and customer service people, adhere to the same standards that you would in the home office.

Play #78: Box Above Your Weight

Similar to the way business initially unfolded in the United States, most of our initial business in Europe stemmed from new technology companies. No deal was too small. The first check made out to the Dublin office was for £35.00. The team in Europe framed it and went out to celebrate. The European outpost won customers across the United Kingdom, Germany, and France. After approximately one year in business, we moved from the four-thousand-square-foot office space where we started to Powerscourt House, an exceptional estate on the outskirts of Dublin. The Georgian building dates back to the eighteenth century. Although I admired it, I wondered if an ancient stone castle was the appropriate command center for our future-focused mission. Worse, the big gates at the entrance reminded me of something out of a Monty Python film.

There was a reason we were there, however. At the time, being a dot-com was a serious liability. It was imperative that we appear reputable and established. The new location was widely known and respected—values with which we wanted to be associated in this market. It worked. Our move to this stately locale attracted a lot of publicity. Once again, start-up salesforce.com figured out a way to stretch its shadow.

Later, in 2006, when we outgrew Powerscourt House, we ripped a page from this playbook and moved into another carefully selected space—an office building next door to Microsoft.

Play #79: Scale Without Overspending

We began to grow with bigger customers, and recruited global leadership to help us build an enterprise sales team in Europe. We expanded the sales organization with carefully planned field offices. We were not influenced by the massive multiheadquarters mentality that defined the rest of the industry. We didn't have much revenue yet, so it made sense to spend less on office space and more on marketing and hiring sales professionals to sell directly.

Although our headquarters were in Dublin, the vast majority of our initial customers, press contacts, and analysts were in London, and I wondered if we needed more of a physical presence there. Because real estate was so expensive in central London, we set up a very small and basic office in Camberley, Surrey (about thirty miles outside the city). This allowed us a home base to build team spirit, but it wasn't necessarily the most convenient location, nor did it radiate the right image to reinforce our brand. Since our early days in Europe, I had been camping out in the Mandarin Oriental in London and using the hotel as a virtual office to meet customers. From eight in the morning until midnight, stakeholders would be in and out of my hotel suite. We were able to do this only because we had Internet-based software. In the old on-premise model, companies needed to have expensive computers (servers) close to the customers to run the complex software and to do the demos, forcing them to buy or rent expensive central London offices.

Even with our new office outside London, we continued to operate out of hotels, which saved us money, and by selecting world-class venues we were able to project an image of success. We continued this cycle for many years and use it to this day as we extend to new markets. (Eventually, I moved out of the Mandarin. The bed was uncomfortable, I missed home, and we grew big enough to warrant a central London office of our own.)

As we gained customers across Europe, we hired employees who worked from home (and hotels), and we opened small offices in Germany, Spain, Italy, and other countries once we had established enough demand.

Play #80: Understand Sequential Growth

We have made strategy changes and added new leadership to our European business, but overall, we have continued to run the Europe, Middle East, and Africa (EMEA) region the same way we do in the United States with a bifurcated business model that has corporate sales (selling to the smaller customers) and enterprise sales (selling to the largest customers) running as almost separate businesses. This is not the only similarity. In fact, we have determined a sequential process to growth that we initiated in the United States and adhere to in nearly every market we enter. The system includes entering a country, establishing a beachhead, gaining customers, earning local references, and then making hires. Next, we seek partners, build add-ons, and grow field sales. It is a system that operates as a machine with distinct cogs that work together. The best part is that it is an iterative process that works in almost all markets; or as Doug Farber, who's built our markets in Australia and Asia, says, the ability to "rinse and repeat" is the key to global growth.

Play #81: Uphold a One-Company Attitude Across Borders

The Internet was making the world more homogeneous when it came to IT needs, and the services we were selling were not affected by global boundaries. Therefore, it was our philosophy to keep as much of our model intact as possible and then make tweaks as necessary. Steve Garnett, the chairman of EMEA, liked to say that our mantra was to build saleforce.com *in* Europe, not to build something entirely new called saleforce.com Europe. We found that a shared vision across borders became the connective tissue of our geographically scattered company.

Our U.S. brand is about success, scrappiness, and customer centricity. Our international PR and marketing strategies embrace those same values. Similarly, our brand is about our unique 1-1-1 integrated philanthropic model, so the foundation has a presence in each of our global offices. Staying true to those values and maintaining a consistent vision have allowed us to extend our message into new markets and even change the way enterprise software companies work.

Admittedly, not everything about our brand was immediately or entirely well received. Our European team was less than eager to participate in the yoga classes or to get massages at off-site worldwide strategy meetings. The Hawaiian shirts were difficult for the Europeans as well. I bought the team shirts at Tommy Bahama so that they could participate in Aloha Fridays during their U.S. visit, and they pledged to continue the tradition in Ireland. Fergus later told me that wearing these shirts during the day in Dublin made him look as if he'd been at a stag party and forgot his way home. "Hawaiian shirts belong significantly west of Ireland," he decided.

Perhaps not everything about salesforce.com was transferable to Europe. It was a good lesson—and one that helped us prepare for building a salesforce.com that would succeed in Japan.

Play #82: Follow Strategy, Not Opportunity

Around the time we first expanded into Europe, we also embarked on building a presence in Japan. I had loved working in Japan when I was at Oracle and had always considered salesforce.com's international focus on Japan a high priority. It was the second-largest IT market in the world, and I knew that Japanese businesses could benefit from our service.

We had long been prepared to enter this market. Salesforce.com had released a Japanese version for trial use at the same time the product was commercially launched in the United States. We also invested in hosting Asian visitors and sharing our End of Software vision with them. Those meetings were a fantastic way to learn about the market in Japan and the needs of Japanese businesses.

Although we had our eye on Japan, it wasn't until we were approached by a large Japanese company with an opportunity to resell our service in the Japanese market that we suddenly had an immediate impetus to explore building capacity in this country. The offer came from a very famous company, but I knew that didn't necessarily mean that this was the appropriate way to enter the Japanese market.

I called Chikara Sano, the CEO of Oracle Japan and one of my mentors, for guidance. Sano-san had led Oracle's success in Japan and helped create the model for partner engagement that was adopted by Oracle globally. He immediately voiced concern over salesforce.com establishing a close alliance with such a large and established company. "If you start off too deeply with one player, this can limit your options down the road," he warned. Oracle's success, he reminded me, was based on its ability to partner with all companies.

Once a company gets some traction in the United States, it's not uncommon for an overseas corporation to express interest in starting operations in its territory. Always be open to opportunity, but do not sign the first one. It is better to act than to react. Further, steer clear of "exclusive" partnerships. Although such a partnership might offer quick entry into an overseas market, it can also severely stymie growth. (You will be limited if your partner isn't growing at the rate you want.) The wrong partner can be a parasite that depletes your assets.

Play #83: Going Far? Take a Partner. Going Fast? Go Alone.

Although the partner deal on the table was not the right agreement for salesforce.com, we understood that the right partner agreement could help us establish a successful presence in the difficult Japanese market. U.S. companies need the leadership of local experts to steer through Japan's cultural, communication, and business practice issues. Sano-san suggested we connect with Allen Miner, the CEO of SunBridge Corporation, an incubator of IT start-ups in Japan, and consider the company as a joint venture partner.

I found the opportunity to partner with SunBridge very compelling inasmuch as I already knew and trusted Allen. He and I first met in May 1986 when we sat next to each other at an orientation for new Oracle employees. Shortly after Allen started, he was dispatched to Japan to build the business there. Japanese companies embraced the product, and Oracle had a successful IPO. Allen and I collaborated on several projects, including Oracle's first product built from scratch with Japanese language support. Both of us had left Oracle at the same time to pursue our own businesses. It was a fortunate coincidence that our paths had crossed again.

Leverage Local Experts

When building a presence overseas, always leverage local resources — especially local experts. Look for a minority-owner joint venture partner that can be a sounding board. A partner can help attract and recruit talent and bring in other partners and vendors. We looked to our partner to help us get started and operate more smoothly, which allowed us to largely avoid the growing pains that many companies (and therefore their customers) experience.

SunBridge mostly focused on working with local Japanese start-ups, but Allen was excited about the opportunity to build salesforce.com in Japan. We structured a unique joint venture agreement that made salesforce.com Japan an independent entity of salesforce.com in the United States. (Most companies structure themselves in Japan as a subsidiary of the U.S. company, but we believed that to succeed we had to be heavily invested in Japan.) The company was set up so that the U.S.-based salesforce.com was the majority owner and SunBridge also invested. Our plan was to build toward an IPO so that the company could be a national asset with ownership opportunities for employees and the shareholding public.

As an IT incubator, SunBridge was involved from the earliest stages and helped the company develop business and recruit the right players, including the first president of salesforce.com Japan. Akira Kitamura came to salesforce.com with more than twenty-five years of experience in the technology industry. In our first meeting, Kitamura-san revealed that this new on-demand delivery model was a shock to him and was entirely unknown in Japan. Still, he was instantly excited about cloud computing becoming the future model for business applications in Japan. I liked his passionate attitude. The right mind-set makes all the difference between succeeding and failing in an international market.

Kitamura-san initially helped salesforce.com gain customer traction by relying on the personal relationships he had built over many years in the industry. In fact, some customers simply bought the service as a favor to him and never even tried it. Luckily, most of the new clients were eager to experience this new model. As always, salesforce.com targeted the end user—not the person who controlled the budget—and these individuals were impressed by the superior customer management that our service offered.

Play #84: Fine-Tune Your International Strategy

After some time building the business in Japan, we found that Oracle's model—that of using partnerships to sell the service—was not working effectively enough for salesforce.com.

Winning partners was a long process, and we needed a better and faster way to penetrate the market. Although the strategy was unusual in the highly fragmented market of Japan, we decided to go back to our basics and build salesforce.com as we first had in the United States and Europe, through aggressive marketing and a direct sales team. This strategy worked, but we did have to make several adaptations to fit the Japanese market.

We recruited Eiji Uda, a direct-sales genius with 20 years' experience at IBM and the president and CEO of SoftBank Commerce (the largest IT distributor in Japan), as president to help build this capacity. Shortly after Uda-san started, we went from getting one or two media hits a month to getting consistent coverage. The difference: the right positioning. Whenever Uda-san introduced salesforce.com as a global company, he referred to other growing companies, such as Google, Amazon, and eBay. This lesson in associating with the right players turned out to be applicable to our entire business in Japan.

Salesforce.com had already proved the power of customer references and testimony, but we learned that there were specific nuances to succeeding with this strategy in Japan. The secret here wasn't in what was said but in the source. To have the most significant impact, references had to come from Japan's key influencers—very large global customers and government organizations.

Although we understood the necessity of capturing these types of customers, winning the biggest players was not an easy feat. In Japan, the leading companies and government agencies tend to be ultraconservative; it's challenging for a foreign company with a new model to land these mega-accounts. Uda-san defined very specific target accounts, and dedicated resources to go after them. He leveraged his relationships with managers at such large companies as Canon, Hitachi, Mizuho, Nippon Steel, NTT, and Ricoh.

We invited managers at these companies to salesforce.com events, similar to the ones we ran in the United States and Europe. One of the sales managers at Canon took the invitation to Haruo Murase, the president and CEO of Canon Marketing Japan, and explained our service to him. Murase-san, considered one of the most respected sales leaders in Japan, wasn't immediately drawn to our service—in fact, his group was in the process of developing a new system using Oracle software, and he dismissed us as one of the "Internet-related ventures trying to get into the market." As luck would have it, though, he attended our event, and he and I had the opportunity to meet.

We mostly talked about cameras (I'm an enthusiastic photographer) and about Canon, which I find to be one of the most innovative companies in the world. Once I returned to the United States, I sent Murase-san an e-mail seeking the Canon EOS Digital camera, which was just being released and was very difficult to obtain. Murase-san arranged for me to receive one of the first ones. (I still use it; it is amazing.) I kept in touch with Murase-san, and whenever I was in Japan, I visited with him and shared with him the developments in our business. Uda-san spent time with him as well, explaining the benefits of our service and how it could be flexible enough to meet the needs of his various lines of business.

Initially as an experiment, Canon tested our service and a competitor's within one business unit. Much as it did in the United States, the land-and-expand strategy worked in Japan. Before long, we had thousands of Canon employees on salesforce.com, and, according to Murase-san, the service has had a significant impact on those users. "Their attitude changed," he said. "The application made their lives easier."

Our team also approached the Japanese government, knowing that winning such an account would serve as a beachhead for the rest of the country. Points of change in a company are always a prime opportunity for entry, and Japan Post, the country's postal system and savings bank (and the largest financial institution in the world in terms of assets), was in the process of being privatized. Kazuhiko Yoshimoto, then the CIO of Japan Post, had been our customer previously at Mizuho Information Research, and we leveraged that relationship and the success Mizuho had experienced with our service. After Japan Post completed an exhaustive and prudent research process, salesforce.com won the open bidding and secured a deal for five thousand subscriptions. (It later grew to more than seventy thousand subscriptions.) This was a major coup, not only because of the impressive size of the contract but also because the government's selection of salesforce.com validated cloud computing services as an alternative to the traditional model. It also convinced me that the Japanese government is very fair and open to foreign companies with new and innovative ideas.

As Uda-san had predicted, winning Japan Post as a customer captured tremendous media attention. The story made top page of the *Nikkei*, the equivalent of the *Wall Street Journal*, and subsequently we were the subject of more than two hundred news articles on this topic alone. The implementation was also a major success with the customer, which deployed our service to twenty-four thousand post offices nationwide in only three months. The Japan Post win also led to the closing of deals with banks and insurance companies. There was a domino effect from there. Many additional large financial institutions, as well as numerous small and medium-size businesses throughout Japan, standardized on salesforce.com. Whereas we were able to start with smaller companies in the United States and Europe, the top-down model is the way to succeed in Japan, where the largest companies provide the most powerful references.

Play #85: Send Missionaries to Build New Markets

It can be difficult to identify talent overseas, and especially challenging to find people who are a cultural fit with your organization. For this reason, there are incredible benefits to temporarily sending the best people from your headquarters to help establish or grow a new market. These expats—or missionaries, as I call them—are tasked with hiring key people, building up a region, and ultimately finding a local executive as their replacement. Although initially, perhaps naively, I thought that such a mission could be accomplished in eighteen months, we've found that it can take closer to thirty-six months.

Having seen the missionary strategy work in other regions, I asked Carl Schachter, who was running the western half of North America's field sales operations, to become the COO of Japan. To Carl, my request seemed out of the blue. He had never lived outside California, and although he spoke Spanish fluently, he did not speak a word of Japanese. This was an idea to which I had given much careful thought, though, and something I believed would work.

In any business, it's vital to keep things dynamic. One way of doing that is by offering talented executives new challenges. Carl was ready for such an opportunity, and the business in Japan needed an operations leader who intimately knew our business and could facilitate communications with headquarters. I also believed that there would be a multitude of benefits to adding a second leader at the top. It can be an effective way to introduce different points of view, drive dialogue, and incite innovative thinking.

I initially offered Carl the opportunity over e-mail, which I sent on a Sunday night. Although some people might disagree with this communication method for significant matters, I find e-mail to be a very effective way to introduce an idea and prompt decision making. In this case, Carl had time to think without being put on the spot, and I was able to arrange to meet with him in person the following day.

"What do you think of Japan?" I asked when he came into my office.

"I've never been," Carl replied.

"I think you should go. You'll know when you get off the plane if it's right for you."

Carl didn't know when he got off the plane (although he did note that the ground was so clean you could eat off of it). After visiting our office, experiencing the efficiency of public transport, and enjoying the energy of Tokyo, he and his family decided to take a risk and upend their lives in California and move to Japan.

Having two leaders at the top worked: Uda-san had the ability to concentrate fully on the Japan market—the "international" side of our business—while Carl, someone intimate with our culture, focused on consistency with headquarters. This is the "global" side of the business, which determines how the international office fits in with the global company. Carl recently left Japan and moved to a new post in Europe. The end goal is always for the international business to be run by local leaders.

However, during the earlier stages of international expansion, tapping two leaders with different experiences is an effective way to lay the right foundation for a company.

International Versus Global Leadership

At many multinational companies, there is a common presumption that headquarters always has it right. Of course that's not always the case. It is the responsibility of the CEO of a global company to put highly qualified people in place in international outposts — and to trust their decisions.

International leaders are specialists in their local markets. They are advisers who are aware of the area's history, culture, laws, buying behaviors, and customs. They know best how to serve their country and region.

Global leaders are executives who specialize in ensuring that international offices fit within the rest of the company. A combination of each of these leaders is essential.

Play #86: Handle Global Disputes with Diplomacy (aka Light and Love)

Salesforce.com always considered Japan a unique market, not a launch pad to the rest of Asia. In fact, our entry in the rest of Asia didn't start in Asia at all, but in Australia. Many U.S. companies use Australia as a gateway. The demographics are similar to those in the United States, the market is made up of early adopters, and the similar time zone and close proximity to Asia make it easy to do business with the rest of the region.

By the time San Francisco–based executive Doug Farber approached me with a business plan outlining a formal foray into Australia and then Asia, we had already won several Australian customers, including one of the country's leading telecom companies and best-known brands. With a burgeoning roster of customers and an understanding of the Australian market (as well as Doug's noteworthy attempt at an Australian accent), it seemed it was time to enter this country.

Although sharing certain cultural sensibilities and having large customers as local references gave us an edge, we knew that setting up shop in a new region would be challenging. Still, we never anticipated the situation that soon arose—and nearly made our launch in Oz impossible.

The day before Doug was scheduled to board a plane as our first missionary in Australia, we received an ominous letter from the legal department of a large Australian company—called SalesForce. SalesForce Australia claimed we were infringing on its registered trademark, and it raised concerns about brand confusion and potential damages. The threatening letter demanded we cease operating under the salesforce name.

This was a gigantic problem. Trademark infringement is a notoriously sticky subject in Australia—and one that can cost companies huge sums of money.

Additionally, SalesForce Australia was an intimidating company to have as an adversary. It had been in the market running outsourced call centers since 1994 and had established a name for itself by working with such huge customers as Hewlett-Packard and BMW. In an effort to prepare for the worst outcome—having to enter the market under a different name—we trademarked the name sforce. I did not, however, want to have to use the alternate name. Salesforce.com had achieved strong brand recognition in the United States and in Europe. Rebranding in Australia and Asia would cause us to forfeit the enormous value we had worked so hard to achieve.

After both of our companies' legal departments failed to resolve the trademark issue, Kevin Panozza, the founder and managing director of SalesForce Australia, decided we'd exhausted the process with lawyers and that it was time to "go direct." It wasn't long before I found myself on the telephone with my Australian counterpart.

Doug had expressed concern that the discussion had the potential to turn ugly. I knew that wouldn't happen. Contrary to what you see in the movies, aggressive and heated conversations are not the way business disputes are best conducted—or resolved. Besides, I had practiced yoga that morning and was prepared to remain peaceful.

Kevin Panozza also knew that the "nice guys finish last" mantra was an antiquated business philosophy. He wasn't interested in allowing the situation to escalate. A great and iconoclastic CEO, Kevin had built a successful company that was rooted in being different from traditional corporations. It was consistently recognized as one of the best places to work in Australia, an especially impressive achievement in an industry traditionally marred by high attrition. The company was known for a culture that embraced freedom of expression, employee recognition, green practices, and Beach Day, which rivaled our own beloved Aloha Fridays. The more I learned, the more I realized that our two salesforces were soul mates. These two companies were meant to meet.

Kevin and I immediately bonded. Each of us wanted to resolve this situation quickly—and limit the legal bills. "How can we work together?" I asked.

As entrepreneurs—and therefore optimists at heart—we knew there had to be an opportunity here. We determined that there were ways for us to partner, refer customers, and collaborate. We decided that there was ample room for both companies in Australia. No one wanted long, drawn-out negotiations, so we agreed to draft a one-page document that addressed our partnership. I told Kevin I wanted "light and love" in the document, and as a kindred spirit who frequently mentions "harmony and balance," he immediately understood.

Perhaps the best part of this story is that it didn't end with the signing of that document. SalesForce Australia, like our company, understood the benefits of giving back to our local communities. Kevin and I pledged to take the amount that our companies could have spent on litigation and instead donate it to establish a young people's development center in Laos. We ultimately won SalesForce as a very important customer after it was acquired by another company, Salmat.

With the right outlook, I've found, it's possible to transform a losing situation into a very lucky break.

How to Write Contracts with Light and Love (or, What the Lawyers Don't Tell You)

A well-drafted contract with "light and love" is a one-page document that is bulletproof and executed perfectly — with as little legal language as possible. The brilliance of this document is in its brevity.

Anyone — not just the legal team — should be able to understand this contract. The key is that it is tight enough to be binding, but loose enough to give latitude so that each party can operate freely.

Once you have such a document, get it executed as quickly as possible! Time quells enthusiasm and leaves you vulnerable to potential risks.

The light-and-love philosophy is not appropriate for every situation; there are plenty of circumstances where a detailed contract is prudent and necessary. However, we find that it makes sense to employ documents with light and love in international situations where we don't want to appear to be litigious Americans and we want to build a strong relationship with the partner or vendor. Sometimes overseas companies (especially in Asia) are overwhelmed by the legal practices of their U.S. counterparts, and they find it refreshing for a U.S. company to take a lighter approach.

Remember, you are entering a new country and must be accommodating to make the right impression. The spirit and philosophy of your approach are paramount: When you enter someone's home, do you ask if you should take your shoes off, or do you put your feet up on the coffee table? Always be sensitive and diplomatic in your approach, and you will be better received.

Play #87: Edit an Overarching Outlook

It was not long before we exploded in Australia. The Australians appreciate a spirit of irreverence, and customers liked the disruptive model we were selling—and the audacious way we were doing it. The free trial, the messaging we had already honed, and the tactics we had previously perfected all worked beautifully in Australia.

It was time to extend into Asia. The region provided an exciting opportunity. More than half of the world's population is there, and the area holds vast promise for growth. At the same time, this region—with its diverse markets, distinct political systems, and myriad cultural barriers—presented giant challenges. As companies before us had found, these markets were diabolically difficult to crack.

Understanding the great deal of time that this would require, and needing to mitigate the risks, we established Australia as the locomotive engine for Asia-Pacific. With a strong currency and buying cycles similar to those in the United States, Australia was a place to gain traction, leverage success, and from which to run marketing, operations, and sales capacity.

Although this "nucleus" strategy was the model many U.S. companies had used, we found parts of it to be flawed. While we had people specifically dedicated to the Asia-Pacific market, most of the office's bookings continued to come from Australia. Furthermore, we realized that what was turning the wheel in Australia (the same model we had used in the United States and Europe) was not similarly moving the rest of Asia. We were accustomed to looking at regions rather than distinct countries with their own local ways of doing business. In Asia, where countries are farther apart in both proximity and ideology than they are in continental Europe, an overarching outlook didn't work.

On the simplest level, Sydney was geographically too far from our target to serve as a real command center. It was a nine-hour flight to Bangkok, a twelve-hour flight to Beijing, and a fifteen-hour flight to Delhi. We were closer to our destination than ever before, yet both physically and metaphorically, we were still too far away.

We needed an office in the heart of Asia-Pacific. Singapore, an English-speaking international business center that offered aggressive economic incentives, provided us with a prime place from which to target the large developing (and geographically equidistant) markets of China and India. The diverse talent pool was also a compelling draw. Technology companies have historically centered their Asia-Pacific operations in Singapore, making the area rich with tech-savvy talent. Furthermore, the city-state's high standards of education and emphasis on bilingual or trilingual skills meant that candidates were often fluent in three or more languages, making them valuable across various geographies.

The Overseas Pull

Satellite offices often prove to be a great place to get your foot in the door. Oftentimes, large corporations will try something new in an office overseas and, if it works, deploy it on a larger scale. We initially won many multinational companies out of Europe or Australia, and later expanded beyond those regions.

Just as we had in the United States and in Europe—and despite what our competitors did—it made sense to start with corporate sales in Asia. It was possible to target, and win, smaller companies without having people on the ground in each country. Aaron Katz, who had international experience on his resume and several years' experience building our business in the United States (and who had been one of our first users), moved from California to bring salesforce.com sales know-how to Singapore. He spent the first six months recruiting star salespeople from Microsoft, Oracle, and Siebel who were working in Bangalore, Hong Kong, Mainland China, and Korea. We relied on these local experts to teach us everything about pricing, positioning, and marketing in their respective countries. We taught them about how we worked, so that ultimately they could bring it back to the markets they knew best.

Unlike the way the rest of the industry operated (where dozens of people are hired in each country and largely neglected when it comes time to sell the product), we brought every new sales hire to Singapore, where they could be closely managed by salesforce.com executives. From that central location, they would also be able to absorb our culture.

Initially it was challenging to convince successful salespeople to move to Singapore. Americans change jobs much more frequently than people in other parts of the world. In Asia, it was considered a great risk for someone to leave a stable job at an established software company and bet on an unheard-of company in an unknown industry. It was an even greater risk for them to leave their homes and uproot their lives for it. It turned out, however, that taking this risk was exactly what later spurred our success. The candidates we convinced to take this huge leap of faith were progressive thinkers who were drawn to the cloud computing model. Moving to a new location made them emotionally invested. With so much at stake, they felt they needed to be successful. Their commitment to success made our customers successful—and that's what has made us successful in the region.

Our corporate sales team in Singapore relied on the same high-velocity corporate sales engine (segmenting the markets, selling to executives, and targeting high-tech and financial services companies) that we had used in other regions. We did, however, ultimately alter our centralized approach to better suit the Asia-Pacific market.

Instead of basing the entire corporate sales organization in Singapore for the long term, we established corporate sales satellites, or "tentacles," that reached into specific markets in order to recognize the diversity of the region and address the unique needs of these countries. After approximately eighteen months of working in Singapore, we found that our transplanted talent was ready to return to their native countries, taking with them what they had learned. The expansion cycle continues as they work as missionaries to further ensure our success in new markets.

Play #88: Bring Old Tricks to New Regions

Although the model that worked in North America and Europe needed to be tweaked, many of the fundamental pieces have worked throughout the world. For example, we have always invested in building market awareness and demand before we build a physical presence. In addition, we've seeded the market with corporate sales, which is easier to start and experiences shorter sales cycles. Corporate sales also proved to tap into a great market: China and India are driven by small and midsize companies.

We discovered that it was possible to recycle some of the same marketing tactics we'd used elsewhere. We also learned the importance of doing due diligence to make sure our efforts would work in a new market, but we learned that lesson the hard way. A few years ago, I was invited to deliver the keynote address at an industry event sponsored by the Infocomm Development Authority of Singapore. I was honored; Michael Dell of Dell and John Chambers of Cisco had previously participated in this Distinguished Infocomm Speakers series. It also served as an excellent opportunity to introduce our AppExchange to developers in Singapore and share with a six-hundred-person audience salesforce.com's vision for a "software-free" future.

We knew that we needed to do something unexpected to tell our story. With that goal in mind, we revived the mock protest marketing stunt from our early days in the United States. We hired more than fifty people and outfitted them in NO SOFTWARE T-shirts and sandwich boards. They carried signs saying, "We Demand: On-Demand" and "Freedom (from Software)" to further support our cause. The "protesters" and our local team enthusiastically demonstrated outside the event center, stirring up curiosity and excitement.

Whereas a protest had previously proved a provocative—and effective—way to introduce ourselves in the United States, protests were viewed differently in the tightly controlled city-state of Singapore. Organized protests, public speeches, and demonstrations are quite rare there. In fact, they are banned unless they are approved by the government or take place in a certain area. Five minutes before I was scheduled to go on stage, the police came and threatened to shut down the whole event. The fun was curtailed, and it was unclear whether or not I'd be able to deliver my address.

The police did break up the protest, but no one was arrested, and I was still allowed to give my keynote. I wouldn't want to relive the experience, and we must always aim to fully understand cultural nuances and how they might affect our efforts, but in hindsight I realize that even despite the gaffe, the stunt was a success. Our message was delivered to a massive audience—and in a style no one would forget. We had made it clear: salesforce.com was the disruptive technology company in the region. That message was validated and reiterated in many newspaper headlines and photos. It was such effective marketing, in fact, that it inspired other companies in Singapore to stage mock protests (which similarly attracted the ire of authorities, but won a storm of publicity).

Don't Confuse Common Values with Common Practices

Stay true to your vision, but do *not* confuse vision with business methods and processes.

It is wise to coordinate high-level marketing globally, such as The End of Software, but big ideas don't always render identical actions and practices. You must appreciate the cultural sensitivities of each market. Whereas the mock protest worked in Singapore (with a few caveats), it would be a total flop in Korea, where it is imperative to demonstrate humility and modesty.

Play #89: Don't Use a "Seagull Approach"; the Secret to Global Success Is Commitment

Perhaps the biggest mistake we made as we tried to gain traction in new markets, especially in Asia, was underestimating the importance of real commitment. At first, we believed we could tend to a market by flying in; hosting a week of great events, such as press conferences and parties; and following up from our home office. That practice required a big investment of time and money, and worse, it was perceived negatively as bespeaking a circus-tent mentality. We'd see a spike in sales immediately after an event, but then interest would fade away. The market showed us that customers wanted our commitment all year long. In Asia, business is conducted face-to-face, and anyone with whom we wanted to do business expected to see us a lot more often than we had first planned.

There were sensitivities to what Doug Farber, one of our first missionaries and now vice president of operations in Asia-Pacific, calls "a seagull approach" (swooping in, messing up the place, and flying away). This concern was especially heightened as everyone remembered the dot-com debacle and the disastrous impact it had in Asia. Silicon Valley companies, flush with billions in market cap, had aggressively expanded across the globe and rushed to hire talent in Asia—only to go out of business a few months later. The experience understandably soured people against dot-coms and foreign investment in general.

We had to demonstrate that we were interested in a long-term commitment by building a sustained presence. We found various ways to increase our commitment to the region, such as building our first international data center in Singapore to better support our growing Asian customer base. We also built a network operations center to monitor the uptime of the three data centers, which required additional facilities and headcount and therefore a significant investment in the region. We've grown the foundation locally, and our employees have made lasting contributions, including helping introduce and establish a basketball focus at Special Olympics Singapore. In addition, growing corporate and field sales offices in several countries has helped our company foster goodwill.

In every relationship, in every market, commitment counts. A company must consider all the ways to become a local asset.

PART 8

The Finance Playbook
How to Raise Capital, Create a Return, and Never Sell Your Soul

Play #90: Don't Underestimate Your Financial Needs

There's no doubt that securing seed capital can be one of the most challenging and stressful aspects of starting a business. To be successful as an entrepreneur, you must passionately believe in your idea and the ability to execute it—and be willing to put a lot on the line. Often that means placing a huge personal financial bet on the venture. Giving up a paycheck and pouring savings into a new business are intimidating, and often they're not even enough. This was the situation I found myself in as we began to grow salesforce.com.

I seeded salesforce.com with $6 million, which I had saved from working at Oracle and earned through my investments in technology companies, but the rapidly growing company required more capital than I had expected. Unlike other software companies that charge big up-front costs for their products and use these checks to finance the company, we were only charging a small fee every month. That model meant that we needed significant capital to stay afloat and grow.

The discovery of insufficient funds is not an unusual one—there's a well-known adage that suggests everything takes twice as long and costs twice as much as you'd expect. That might be hyperbole, but we were certainly not alone in underestimating what it would cost to build our business. Misjudging the necessary financial resources can be a fatal mistake; according to one study, 79 percent of small businesses cited "starting out with too little money" as one of their causes of collapse.[1] We did not want to become one of those failures.

In the beginning, I wasn't too worried. I thought our financial woes would be easily answered by a windfall investment from a venture capital firm. This was still the frothy dot-com era, and it didn't seem all that difficult to raise money. After all, one company raised enough venture capital money to spend more than $1 million to place a sock puppet in an ad during the Super Bowl. I had connections to big-name venture capitalists, which was helpful because it's difficult to win a venture capitalist's attention with a cold pitch. VC financing made sense for a business like ours—a hypergrowth Internet technology company looking for a substantial multimillion-dollar investment.

It turned out that I was wrong in my assumption. VC after VC turned us down. It wasn't challenging to secure meetings, but those meetings did not go very well. We could not come to an agreement on the price, and I believed that the VCs were significantly undervaluing our company. Most of all, it was evident that many of the people with whom we met just didn't understand what we were doing. A few told us that they believed in networked computing—not our disruptive "no software" model.

Although it was disheartening not to be able to raise venture capital, I knew that I wasn't the first entrepreneur to be told that a good idea wouldn't work. MGM reportedly told Walt Disney that Mickey Mouse would never be a hit because a giant mouse on the screen would terrify women. And for every seemingly insignificant idea that was venture financed (and there were some harebrained ideas) there were others, including Cisco, E*TRADE, and Starbucks, that had been passed on at some point.[2] Rejection from venture capitalists was not enough of a reason to consider getting out of our business or even changing our business (only 10 percent of venture-backed technology companies ultimately become successful),[3] but it was the impetus to find a new financing strategy—and to find one quickly!

Play #91: Consider Fundraising Strategies Other Than Venture Capital

In looking for a new way to grow our business, I reached out to my friends and colleagues—people who believed in me and my ideas. This was hardly an unconventional strategy. In the U.S., entrepreneurs provide on average about two-thirds of startup capital and after that look to family, friends, work colleagues, and strangers—not venture capital firms—to provide the remainder of the investment capital. (Of that group, research shows that family and friends provide 78 percent of the total.)[4] Raising capital from private investors is not as simple as knowing people with resources, though. It's pivotal to find people who are visionaries.

I was very fortunate to have friends, colleagues, and mentors who believed in young entrepreneurs and start-up businesses as the source of innovation, and like me, they supported that belief by investing their resources. Magdalena Yesil, a great entrepreneur and friend, put in $500,000. Larry Ellison invested $2 million. With Magdalena's help, I continued to develop this piecemeal funding strategy by creating a list of potential investors and a target of how much capital we needed to raise.

Treat Friends and Family Investors Professionally

She might be your friend, or your grandmother, but treat her as an investor. This is not only because it's respectful but also because not doing so could come back to bite you. If you target larger investors later, the legal teams at these organizations will scrutinize your capitalization structure, and any previous negligence will cost you.

Apply professional standards in structuring and documenting all investments. Create a plan that includes formal projections and an assessment of when investors will see a return. This reminds investors why they chose to invest in you in the first place!

It was incredible to discover that many of the people in my immediate circle were enthusiastic supporters of our mission; I realized that piecemeal funding through my friends and network was a winning fundraising strategy. Investing in someone is a big bet, and it's a lot easier to persuade someone who already believes in you than it is to convince someone you've just met. The founders invested; Halsey Minor, the founder of CNET, made a significant investment; Arjun Gupta, a venture capitalist (and the friend with whom I went on the pivotal trip to India), personally invested; Igor Sill, legendary technology investor and the head of the search firm GenevaGroup, gave us money; as did Ted Waitt of Gateway, William Hambrecht of Hambrecht & Quist, Stratton Sclavos of VeriSign, and many others. We did eventually receive venture funding—$15.5 million from Attractor Partners—likely because founding partner Gigi Brisson had been a friend for fifteen years and believed in my capabilities. In total, we raised $65 million over five rounds of funding from 1999 to 2002.

Ultimately, our unconventional financing model turned out to be a better strategy than venture capital, sometimes called "vulture capital," a method which would have required us to give away a hefty stake of ownership and control. It also profoundly affected my role in building the company. More than two-thirds of the time, VCs replace founding CEOs. It's not really a surprise. From the VC's point of view, who would be a smarter bet? A first-time CEO, or someone the VC knows who has a track record? I understood that reality, but I didn't like it.

The financing strategy we were forced to pursue worked, and now the venture capitalists that turned us down are the ones with regrets. Everyone who invested in the initial rounds has made a significant return. (Larry's $2 million is worth more than $200 million, for example.)

Play #92: Use Internet Models to Reduce Start-Up Costs

Although the strategy we used to finance salesforce.com was somewhat unconventional in 1999, especially when VC money was flowing like Niagara Falls, it's becoming more and more plausible today for companies to start up without venture capital. Thanks to the falling cost of hardware, overseas coders, and on-demand services, start-ups need less capital to get off the ground.

Bootstrapping through Internet models is a viable way to build and run a company and an attractive and appropriate solution for a challenging financial climate. There are now an increasing number of start-ups that have built applications on PaaS offerings, run their services on external servers, and manage their businesses entirely in the cloud. There are also more ways to secure the capital they do need.

Angel investors, or individuals who provide start-up capital (usually in the few-hundred-thousand-dollar range), are becoming more common and more organized. The number of angel investments has always outnumbered the number of VC deals by at least ten to one, says Jeffrey Sohl, the Director of the Center for Venture Research. Although the amount invested declined during the economic fallout of 2008, the number of deals has stayed constant and angels are just as interested as ever and still actively investing, according to research released by the Center.[5] There are local angel networks in most cities, and it's likely that your accountant or attorney already knows angels. So-called superangels—successful entrepreneurs who invest larger amounts, often in the multimillions, in start-ups—also offer experience and insight as VCs would, but they are known to be friendlier.

Play #93: Set Yourself Up Properly from the Beginning, Then Allow Your Financial Model to Evolve

Although we had initially thought that a customer's attraction to our service hinged on a no-contract "pay by the drink" premise, this model was crippling us financially. In retrospect, it made little sense to deliver a great service to customers, pay salespeople their annual commission for winning the account, and then collect payment at the end of each month. We made a critical change to our financial structure by evolving to a subscription model with annual contracts. In our new "deferred revenue" model, we collect the cash up front and report the revenue as the service is delivered. It has been an ideal model to scale, and because we have an annuity, we are released from the end-of-quarter pressures that plague companies using the perpetual model. Although this is how all SaaS companies operate today, at the time it was not easy to implement, and it required a massive restructuring of our company.

In some ways, our new business model simplified matters, as we no longer had to send a bill every month, but the transformation of our service also required operational changes that seeped into every department. We had to convince customers to pay in advance, and that had ramifications on sales, marketing, and, of course, finance.

The changes required that we build a formal process to execute contracts and manage renewals. These financial house-keeping systems allowed us to better predict revenue and become a more stable company. Further, we anticipated that our next round of financing would be through an IPO, and these formal systems served to demonstrate to Wall Street that we could define—and meet—projections.

Play #94: Measure a Fast-Growing Company on Revenue, Not Profitability

In a fast-growing business like salesforce.com, we needed to focus on revenue growth and capturing market share. To do so, everyone had to be measured on finding new customers and expanding sales with existing customers. We determined to measure everyone on revenue—not profitability. Most accountants would disagree with this philosophy: "Revenue is vanity; profit is sanity," they often say. I'm not suggesting that profits aren't necessary, pivotal, and even beautiful. It's just not appropriate to stress profits over revenue in the beginning when you are starting out and building a company.

Here's why: if you turn to measuring people on profit too soon and during high-growth stress, then they start to think about how they can cross-charge other functions or divisions (on office space, computers, people) so that they can make a quarterly bonus. They do this instead of focusing outside the company on increasing the revenue line. Further, there is a danger that measuring on profit can prevent managers from sharing their talent with other departments because they feel as if they are "paying for them" and bearing the brunt of the cost.

This creates the wrong kind of behavior and culture, and is not a way that allows an organization to thrive.

Play #95: Build a First-Class Financial Team

As part of the internal restructuring, it became clear that we needed someone who could help lead us through this transition and help us scale. In 2002, we had about $25 million in annual revenue, and I began to query my network. I asked my neighbor in Napa Valley, Steve Cakebread, the CFO of Autodesk, a billion-dollar software business, if he could recommend any CFO candidates.

Steve visited me in the salesforce.com office, and I gave him a demonstration of our service. Although Steve had been at large technology companies his whole career, including many years at the Silicon Valley pioneer Hewlett-Packard, he was immediately captivated by what our small company was doing, but then he told me that he couldn't think of someone who would be a good CFO for our company. Then he said, "Why not me?"

I didn't have to give this opportunity much thought. "Yes," I immediately replied. I was ecstatic to have a world-class CFO help build our company as we aimed to evolve from a start-up challenger into a market leader.

Right away, Steve and I sat down in our conference room and discussed the company's future. We discussed our long-term goals. My goals were to

- Win one million subscribers
- Become a $1 billion company

- Achieve profitability
- Go public on the NASDAQ

"Okay," said Steve, believing that it was possible to reach all these aims. "But one change: instead of going public on the NASDAQ, let's trade on the NYSE."

Play #96: Be Innovative and Edgy in Everything You Do—Except When It Comes to Your Finances

It was always our goal for salesforce.com to go public. Most companies go public to raise cash, which they use to expand, acquire companies, or retire debt, but this was not our impetus. First and foremost, we wanted credibility. We had built the SaaS industry, and now we wanted to be the first SaaS company to go public.

An IPO would market—and endorse—our service, our company, and our industry. It's like a Good Housekeeping seal of approval for companies, and the trust it instills can help retain talent, recruit leaders, expand business relationships, and reassure customers.

Steve's suggestion to trade on the NYSE went hand in hand with this reasoning. "We are in San Francisco, so people already think we're flakey; and we're a dot-com, and those are going away quickly," he said. "We need the credibility and the panache of the NYSE brand: it's traditional, old-line, well established. It's the antithesis of salesforce.com."

The NYSE was another way to alter our image. We were new and edgy and innovative in everything we did—except fiscal matters, in which it was best to align with ways that were established, proven, and successful.

Taking a company public, as any entrepreneur in the process quickly learns, is not about the one glorious moment when you ring the bell at the NYSE. It entails months, or more likely years, of preparation. Going public was not just about changing our model, improving our cash flow, and bringing on an experienced CFO. It was about strengthening our entire team with talented people who could help us prepare for the transition.

We recruited a finance leader, Joe Allanson, who had worked with Steve in corporate finance at Autodesk and had experience at another Fortune 500 company and in the audit advisory practice at a big accounting firm. As finance leader, Joe would help us prepare for the IPO and help us establish revenue recognition practices, GAAP accounting policies, and SEC reporting—all procedures and policies that were new to our privately held company. There were many internal controls and processes to put in place to comply with the Sarbanes-Oxley requirements for financial reporting, to which we would be accountable as a public company. We hired Ernst & Young, one of the largest professional services firms in the world, as our external accountant, and a well-known law firm to help us manage the vast array of legal requirements.

The changes required discipline and the embracing of a different mind-set to ensure that we were able to make this transition. We prepared so that salesforce.com would internally function as a public company before it actually was a public company. For example, one year before we went public, we built an internal audit department to check the processes and procedures. Most companies establish this the quarter after they go public, but we wanted to demonstrate to investors that unlike the rebel strategies we applied elsewhere in business, our approach to finances was extraordinarily conservative. This was, after all, during the period of the highly publicized scandals of Enron and Tyco. We knew that we had a great business model that would attract investors, but it was more important than ever to prove that we also had good discipline.

By the time we filed to go public in December 2003, we had almost $100 million in revenue. Many companies before us had gone public with $30 to $40 million in revenue, but the game had changed entirely by our time. After the dot-com bubble burst, there was a lockdown on IPOs. As the market began to recover, companies needed to have significant revenue and be profitable to go public. At this time, two companies were being hyped as being able to re-ignite the high-tech IPO market. One was Google; the other was salesforce.com.

The salesforce.com IPO was viewed as a litmus test for a new business model, so everyone became interested in the deal. Both the NASDAQ and the NYSE competed for the business, trying to lure us by promising such perks as advertising spots or hosted luncheons on the trading floor. There were great companies on the NASDAQ, such as Intel and all the best Internet companies, but the NYSE offered its authority as well as the opportunity to be the first dot-com on that exchange. Those advantages were unbeatable.

We were unsure of what our NYSE ticker would be, and we spent a great deal of time trying to come up with what would best represent our company (companies on the NYSE have historically had one, two, or three letters; companies on the NASDAQ have had four or five). I was debating a few choices, but not sold on any, when one of our bankers came to me and said, "What about 'CRM'?"

Right away we knew it would be a home run. At the time, we wanted to be in the customer relationship management, or CRM, business. Our name was salesforce.com, which was slightly misleading because we did so much more than SFA. We did not want to change our name, though, as that would have had significant logistical and branding consequences. Instead, we used the ticker symbol to help us broadcast the bigger message we had for the future.

We learned early on in the process that even the potential to go public gave us both the appearance and the reality of stability, which resonated with prospective customers. Shortly after we filed with the SEC, Automatic Data Processing (ADP), the giant administrative solutions company that handles payroll for most of America's companies, chose to place an order with us over the market leader. This was one of the most important customer wins in our history, as ADP demanded a highly secure environment. ADP's adoption of our service validated the security of our system.

Internally, the IPO had a wildly invigorating effect. Employees were ecstatic about the future. There was great camaraderie at the company, with both a deep respect for the old-timers who had built the company and an appreciation for the newcomers who had helped us prepare for this next stage. When Joe Allanson came in on the day we filed—looking uncharacteristically disheveled, having spent the night at the financial printers readying the regulatory paperwork for the SEC—he was welcomed as a superhero.

Although filing to go public was an incredible emotional high, there were some lows that soon followed. It's routine to hear from the SEC with questions about the filing, and we heard from the Commission in January, a month after we filed. Because we were the first SaaS company to go public, our model was new to the regulators, and our offering was viewed as one that would set a precedent for all SaaS companies. The federal regulators asked many questions about our deferred cost model, specifically the basis for deferring sales commissions. (Traditional software companies immediately expense the full cost of their sales commissions.) The SEC inquiry delayed the IPO, which was originally anticipated for early March. Before long, the issues were leaked to the press.

After weeks of delay, a trip to Washington, DC, to meet face-to-face with a senior partner from Ernst & Young, and the partner's discovery of a recorded precedent for our model, the SEC accepted our point of view and accounting. This model is the only way a highly involved software subscription model can work, and it's in line with generally accepted accounting principles. It also allows a better evaluation of profitability and performance because it clearly delineates how much is spent to earn revenue. Months later, accounting firms began to publish our accounting for deferred commissions in their literature. And then years later, Ernst & Young issued a revenue recognition position paper for SaaS companies, which covers the key concepts and issues that arise in determining when and how to recognize revenue. Now all SaaS companies do their accounting the way we do.

Although the SEC's scrutiny of our accounting principles was a serious challenge for our company, it did not sour investors on the salesforce.com deal. The extensive interest led us to the finance industry's version of a "bake-off," in which ten investment banks came to our office to pitch for our business.

Our goal was to find the right bank to underwrite our deal as well as the right group of research analysts—people who understood our company and its place in our rapidly growing industry.

Play #97: When It Comes to Compliance, Always Play by the Rules

In the final weeks before the IPO, Steve Cakebread, the I-banking team, and I had scheduled trips to major finance centers in Europe and the United States to visit the top institutional money managers and other investors and give them our thirty-minute pitch. We were at the start of the road show and had just arrived in Washington, DC, when we got a disturbing phone call from one of our advisers: "There's a problem; the IPO is being held up."

As the shock subsided and the weight of that statement set in, we learned that the SEC believed that we had violated securities law by promoting our offering before the regulators had declared it ready to go. This accusation referred to a *New York Times* profile about me, which had run a few days before. The regulators believed that my participation in the article violated the "quiet period," which restricts management and insiders of companies that are going public from hyping their IPO or disclosing any information to the public that is not included in its IPO prospectus.

We had been conscious of the SEC's quiet-period rules, which made it very challenging to engage in our ordinarily high level of PR activities. Sales leads that came to us through publicity were the lifeblood of large parts of our business. We tried hard to maintain the right balance between promoting our services and respecting the rules. I discussed the *New York Times* opportunity with David Schellhase, our general counsel, and he agreed that focusing on our business and the SaaS model was within the letter and spirit of the quiet-period rules. Whenever the reporter asked me about the offering, I declined to comment, saying, "The rules prohibit me from making any statements that would promote my IPO." Reporter Gary Rivlin even wrote that I repeated that statement "whenever the conversation drifted even close to the pending stock offerings."

Other than my declining to comment, I wasn't quoted very much. Although no one at salesforce.com spoke about the upcoming offering, the story focused much more on the IPO than we had anticipated. It was even in the story's headline: "It's Not Google. It's That Other Big IPO."

The attention paid to the IPO during the quiet period caused the SEC to delay the IPO for thirty days to allow any hyperbole stirred up by the *Times* article to subside. A month's delay made us vulnerable to the unexpected, such as a downturn in the economy or a loss of interest on the part of investors who might have wanted to buy our stock. We had worked intensely for this, our employees had made sacrifices and taken pay cuts at precarious points in our history, and all of us had believed that the financial rewards of our efforts were within reach. Instead, we faced a huge new uncertainty.

We overcame this obstacle by working even more closely with the regulators to understand their concerns. At the SEC's request, David ended each day by sending the SEC copies of all the articles mentioning the company that had appeared that day. Ultimately, despite its initial concerns, the SEC was incredibly supportive throughout the quiet period, and the rest of the IPO process went smoothly. I think the regulators understood that the *Times* article had been an honest mistake.

Although painful at the time, in retrospect, the quiet-period violation did not hurt us. In fact, ironically, the SEC's slowing down of the process created far more publicity for the IPO than the single *New York Times* article did. The uproar helped sales, too: we won more leads that month than we had ever had.

Later, Google had a similar problem, although their article was in *Playboy*, not in the *New York Times*. Eventually, the SEC, recognizing that times had changed since the Securities Act of 1933 that put the "gun-jumping" provisions in place, updated its rules in 2005.

Luckily, the issues we experienced did not quell investors' enthusiasm for our IPO. We were the first SaaS company to go public, the first dot-com to go public in several years, and the first dot-com that would trade on the NYSE. Ringing the bell at the NYSE on the morning of Wednesday, June 23, 2004, was one of the most exciting moments of my career. We'd had big plans for this moment, including wearing Hawaiian shirts and hosting a luau to pay homage to our aloha spirit, but we decided that it would be best, given the previous issues, to appear more buttoned up. Playing it straight on the day of our IPO demonstrated the dichotomy that is salesforce.com. We may use nontraditional tactics and aggressive branding, marketing, and communications, but internally, we are run very conservatively.

The elation I felt on the morning we went public lasted long beyond the opening bell. It was incredibly gratifying to watch the stock climb; you can't help but take it very personally. We ended our first day of public trading at $17.20, a 56 percent gain—making salesforce.com the best-performing tech IPO 2004 had seen thus far.

When I walked out of the New York Stock Exchange, I was still reeling with excitement when I nearly collided with a longtime friend, Charlie Moore. Charlie's office is on Wall Street, so the meeting wasn't that surprising, but it was significant. Charlie is the executive director of the Committee Encouraging Corporate Philanthropy (CECP)—an organization that has inspired, mentored, and embraced us. I knew seeing him at that moment was a sign. We had been rewarded financially and were now a public company, but we also had to preserve the ideals of the company we had set out to create. We had to stay true to our core values, especially our philanthropic values.

Play #98: Focus on the Future

There is a lot of heavy lifting in preparing to go public. Then, after you are a public company, everything really changes. Our cash account skyrocketed from $30 million to $150 million, and we needed to build a team to manage it.

Whereas our earlier history had been defined by figuring out how to survive, an entirely different set of standards applies to managing a public company. Overnight, there were vastly more shareholders and a different level of responsibility. Our new focus was on maintaining rapid growth for our investors, while at the same time complying with an alphabet soup of procedures (GAAP, SOX, SEC rules) and corporate policies, local laws, and business values and ethics.

In order to succeed in this next stage in our evolution, we had to continue to put formal systems and procedures into place that would help us scale and grow. One of the most important changes was establishing a worldwide revenue department to maintain tight controls. Revenue restatements are the number-one risk to shareholders and have the greatest potential to derail a company. We hired Meredith Schmidt, who had been at PeopleSoft and KPMG, to direct our new worldwide revenue department. Coming from the old world of enterprise software, Meredith was excited about the power of the multitenancy model, and especially its effect on revenue recognition. She was accustomed to having to defer revenue until professional services were delivered, meaning that enormous license fees of millions of dollars couldn't be recognized until the next quarter. With SaaS, the delivery is nearly immediate and the recognition of revenue can therefore commence just a few days after the contract is signed.

Although Meredith thought that recognizing revenue on a subscription model would be a cinch, she soon discovered that recognizing revenue for a SaaS company came with a whole new set of challenges. Our sales team was selling to the customer constantly. Because we were continually adding new users or innovating new products, it had become common to renegotiate the contracts and create new ones. That turned into an organizational nightmare for managing revenue, and the ambiguity that came from renegotiating made us susceptible to risk. We needed to find a way to define everything up front and standardize the way we did sales contracts. We had to negotiate all the future possibilities ahead of time to guarantee that we got the best terms.

There were SEC guidelines to help determine what we required in order to recognize revenue, but we needed an expert to help explain the guidelines in the context of our business and the different scenarios that could emerge. In an effort to clarify this, Meredith created a fifty-five-page document for the finance and legal departments to serve as a practical guide to revenue, and included frequently asked questions. Meredith's document was designed to illuminate exactly what we could or couldn't do in the sales contracts. For example, could a customer ask for a discount on a product that it was not purchasing at this time? (Yes.) Does the pricing the customer negotiates apply to all of its affiliates? (Yes.) Do we give refunds to the affiliates that paid a higher price? (No, no refunds on revenue that's been recognized.) As a start-up, we had been so focused on survival that we'd adopted an überflexible attitude as a way to please customers and secure deals. As we matured, though, we needed to define the practices that best benefited our company in the long run.

A large part of getting the right procedures in place included proper tax planning—especially planning for future international work. "There is a risk if you don't figure this out beforehand because you will be assessed after," Rafe Brown, who came from Cisco to head up salesforce.com's new tax and treasury department, told us. "This is the first place to hurt yourself." Tax planning was no longer just about being compliant but about becoming tax efficient, something that takes years of planning before you see the benefits.

Play #99: Allow for Change as Your Company Grows

There was a lot to get used to in our new status as a publicly traded company. The Sarbanes-Oxley filings required an army of experts and doubled the amount we had to spend on outside advisers. The *New York Times* article–IPO fiasco taught us an important lesson, and we had to become even more mindful of what we said publicly and when we said it. There were strict rules around releasing quarterly financial results, shareholder meetings, and discussions with investors and analysts. (I was accustomed to speaking with journalists individually and informally, but communicating with Wall Street required speaking with all the analysts at one time, giving them each a chance to bombard me with questions.)

There was a major attitude shift we had to adopt as a public company, and this, perhaps, was the biggest change of all. At each level of growth, adjustments are required; it's the natural process of maturing. That said, growing up isn't always easy, and it's not always fun. It can be tough for a fast-moving entrepreneurial culture to adopt more structure, but bringing outside talent into the organization can make it easier to see what changes are necessary to ensure a smooth transition.

One of the people we recruited to help us scale was Ken Juster, former U.S. undersecretary of commerce and a former senior partner at a major law firm. I knew that there were many exciting opportunities ahead, including possible acquisitions and more international expansion, but such opportunities come with risks. Ken had the experience, judgment, and instincts to help us mitigate the risks and take actions that befit a maturing organization.

Under Ken's guidance, we instituted a series of processes, practices, and programs to help make us more systematic in the way we approached a number of issues. For example, our legal team began to monitor the acceptable degree of risk in customer contracts. Our corporate development team established a disciplined and structured approach to evaluating potential acquisitions, so that we avoided deals that could overextend and distract the company, while we still pursued smaller transactions that would have a significant impact on our growth and strategic evolution. We also became more focused and strategic about our international expansion. And we developed a public policy team, which is unusual for a young company, but was necessary to ensure the right regulatory environment for the emerging SaaS industry.

We also put in place formal procedures and processes for personnel matters, such as stock refresh grants and performance pay raises, which previously had been handled on an ad hoc basis. In addition, our real estate and facilities team began to take a more strategic approach to managing our growth in the real estate market, gradually transitioning us away from being overly concentrated in San Francisco and implementing cost-saving approaches, such as the "hoteling" of office space, in which there are fewer work spaces than employees—a practical adaptation to the flexible and highly mobile nature of the workforce. Finally, we began to focus on a broad assessment of enterprise risks and on measures to mitigate such risks, including the development of business continuity plans.

This overall development of our corporate infrastructure has been one of the keys to our success and our ability to grow rapidly. Of course, all the changes did not necessarily happen naturally. Employees, especially those who had been here for some time, often wanted to do things the old way. As much as I love change, that even included me at times. For example, I was initially hesitant to include some of the tougher provisions in sales contracts. Eventually, however, customers agreed to our demands, and we signed better deals.

Although it took some time, we learned the virtue of patience and holding out for what we believed made the most sense. We learned to be more confident in ourselves, our products, and our company. We learned that how you are treated in the marketplace is a reflection of how you behave.

We've seen the rewards of always taking the long view. Although we've built a company by making rapid decisions and by responding to the ever-changing needs of the market, financial success is not something we achieved through quick actions. It took careful planning, far in advance of where we were at the time. As we've learned, it doesn't make sense to plan for the company you are. You have to plan for the company you want to be.

Think Three Years Out

What you do this year drives success for next year and the year after. You must make investments for the future.

Years ago, we received criticism for spending "too much" on marketing for a $250 million company, but when we were a $250 million company, we weren't thinking like a $250 million company. We were trying to build a bigger company, and the only way to do that was to act like one.

Later, as we neared the $1 billion in revenue mark, we didn't focus on $1 billion in revenue, but what we needed to do to get to $10 billion in revenue.

PART 9

The Leadership Playbook

How to Create Alignment—the Key to Organizational Success

Play #100: Use V2MOM to Focus Your Goals and Align Your Organization

I've always thought that the biggest secret of salesforce.com is *how* we've achieved a high level of organizational alignment and communication while growing at breakneck speeds. While a company is growing fast, there is nothing more important than constant communication and complete alignment. We've been able to achieve both with the help of a secret management process that I developed a number of years ago.

When I was at Oracle, I struggled with the fact that there was no written business plan or formal communication process during our growth phase. In fact, I remember asking

Larry Ellison during my new hire orientation, "What is Oracle's five-year plan?" His response was simple: "We don't have a five-year plan, we barely have a six-month plan." (Even for that, there was no written plan, only a budget.) It was our job to figure it out what Larry wanted on our own.

What I yearned for at Oracle was clarity on our vision and the goals we wanted to achieve. As I started to manage my own divisions, I found that I personally lacked the tools to spell out what we needed to do and a simple a process to communicate it. The problem only increased as the teams that I was managing increased.

I went out to look for help. I sought wisdom from leadership gurus, personal development gurus, and even spiritual gurus. Over time, I realized that many of these seemingly disparate sources shared striking similarities. I looked to employ these common threads in my own work, and over time I developed them into my own management process, V2MOM, an acronym that stands for vision, values, methods, obstacles, and measures. This tool (pronounced "V2 mom") has helped me achieve my goals in my past work and helps make salesforce.com a success. Although there are many leadership paradigms and frameworks available to follow, V2MOM offers a new simplicity. It is easy to digest, unlike other programs that take longer to understand than they do to implement.

V2MOM enabled me to clarify what I was doing and communicate it to the entire company as well. The *vision* helped us define what we wanted to do. The *values* established what was most important about that vision; it set the principles and beliefs that guided it (in priority). The *methods* illustrated how we would get the job done by outlining the actions and the steps that everyone needed to take. The *obstacles* identified the challenges, problems, and issues we would have to overcome to achieve our vision. Finally, the *measures* specified the actual result we aimed to achieve; often this was defined as a numerical outcome. Combined, V2MOM gave us a detailed map of where we were going as well as a compass to direct us there.

Essentially, V2MOM is an exercise in awareness in which the result is total alignment. In addition, having a clarified direction and focusing collective energy on the desired outcome eliminate the anxiety that is often present in times of change.

In the first few weeks of operation at salesforce.com, I suggested that my cofounders and I define a V2MOM and commit it to writing. Although Parker may have thought it was somewhat strange at the time, something made him save the original salesforce.com V2MOM, which I had scribbled on a large American Express envelope. He framed it and gave it to me on the day of our IPO. You can see how it established a foundation for the company—and how it has steered us to date. In a sense, that V2MOM became our business plan.

Many organizations rely on some kind of rubric or tool to help manage their business. Most common are organizational charts, which are used to delineate the structure of an organization. I never liked org charts as a management tool. They are narrow, they don't capture the nuances of an organization, and they aren't empowering for employees. Further, they are static—they don't spur creativity or encourage change. Another tool that many businesses employ are key performance indicators, metrics used to help measure progress, and some companies look at critical success factors for such events as product launches. We don't use any of these at salesforce.com. These metrics are stagnant, and they don't work in today's fast-moving environment, which requires that companies adapt

Salesforce.com's First V2MOM, 4/12/1999

Vision

Rapidly create a world-class Internet company/site for Sales Force Automation.

Values

1. World-class organization
2. Time to market
3. Functional
4. Usability (Amazon quality)
5. Value-added partnerships

Methods

1. Hire the team
2. Finalize product specification and technical architecture
3. Rapidly develop the product specification to beta and production stages
4. Build partnerships with big e-commerce, content, and hosting companies
5. Build a launch plan
6. Develop exit strategy: IPO/acquisition

Obstacles

1. Developers
2. Product manager/business development person

Measures

1. Prototype is state-of-the-art
2. High-quality functional system
3. Partnerships are online and integrated
4. Salesforce.com is regarded as leader and visionary
5. We are all rich

Create Your Own V2MOM

V2MOM has been used to guide every decision at salesforce.com — from those we made in 1999 to the decisions we make today as the largest high-tech employer in San Francisco. I've also introduced it to other business leaders and to musician Neil Young, who uses it to align his goals for LincVolt, his current effort to create a clean-power automobile technology.

The beauty of the V2MOM is that the same structure works for every phase in the life cycle of an organization. We've used it as a business plan for our start-up, and we find the same construct to be effective for outlining the annual goals of a public company.

Think about your overall organizational goals or a present-day challenge within your organization, and discover how you can outline the steps to succeed in your effort through the V2MOM process. You might have more than one answer to each question; be sure to prioritize your answers:

VISION (What do you want?):

_____

VALUES (What's important about it?):

_____

METHODS (How do you get it?):

_____

OBSTACLES (What might stand in the way?):

_____

MEASURES (How will you know when you have it?):

_____

continuously. Organizations that don't adapt have problems in the long run, and these antiquated tools don't inspire constant change.

At salesforce.com, everything we do in terms of organizational management is based on our V2MOM. It is the core way we run our business; it allows us to define our goals and organize a principled way to execute them; and it takes into consideration our constant drive to evolve. The collaborative construct works especially well for a fast-paced environment. It is challenging for every company to find a way to maintain a cohesive direction against a backdrop that is constantly changing, but V2MOM is the glue that binds us together.

Play #101: Use a Top-Down and Bottom-Up Approach

From the very beginning, we've had a V2MOM at salesforce.com, and we've always kept it updated. It is a living document. It's my responsibility to write the V2MOM, and then I work with the rest of the people at our company to make it as accurate as possible. I rewrite the V2MOM every six months, which helps me gain personal clarity as well as communicate with the company.

Immediately after I write the V2MOM, I share it with our top officers (what we call our "President's committee," or "Pcomm") at our weekly meetings and ask for their feedback. Sometimes they love it and sometimes they hate it, but the exercise always ensures a worthy debate. Once everyone comes to an agreement, we bring the V2MOM to our "Core," which is how we refer to our top thirty officers, and we then incorporate their insights.

This process of constant iteration is critical to making the V2MOM accurate as well as to integrate these ideas into our corporate consciousness. One way we truly achieve this is by presenting the V2MOM at our bi-annual global managers' meeting, where we gather our top two hundred fifty officers. We break this group into fifteen teams and ask them to focus on a critical part of the V2MOM. They then present their work back to the whole group. Through this process, our entire management team becomes truly involved in setting the company's direction.

Without a doubt, this process has been our best-kept secret to the fast growth and excellence we have achieved. Reading the Vision statements through a sampling of years illustrates the goals of our company at various points in time. We have been able to reach these goals because our vision—and a way to achieve it—was defined and communicated.

Although we rely on our executives to return from the off-site meeting and introduce the V2MOM to their departments, this top-down approach is not the only way that the messages flow through our organization. We have benefited from involving our employees in this process. With the development of our platform technology, we gained increased opportunities to communicate with—and seek advice from—our employees.

We now collaborate on the corporate V2MOM with all salesforce.com employees through IdeaExchange, a social networking tool that employees use to contribute their ideas as well as promote and comment on others' ideas. Most recently, when our V2MOM went live on IdeaExchange, we received feedback from more than half of the company's employees over a two-week period. I was amazed at the unfiltered view this afforded us. Employees told us what was happening in customer

Vision Statements

1999–Rapidly create a world-class Internet company/site for Sales Force Automation.

2002–Global leadership in proving the "software as service" model driven by an enthusiastic and wildly successful customer community, and energized by world-class employees.

2004–Dominate the software as a service market by doubling our enthusiastic and wildly successful global customer community through flawless execution of our proven model.

2006–Deliver trusted customer and partner success globally, and accelerate our growth as the unrivaled on-demand standard for The Business Web through efficient execution.

2009–Create wildly successful customers, secure every renewal, and grow our customer relationships through the Service Cloud and Force.com. Increase the productivity of every employee and every department, to gain market share and dominate enterprise cloud computing.

support, employee development, and delegation, and suggested ideas to improve our organization. We used their insights to create a better final V2MOM and set the course for our next year.

Although we use one corporate V2MOM to direct salesforce.com, V2MOMs cascade throughout the entire organization. We've created a system whereby each executive builds his or her own V2MOM from the corporate V2MOM, and then his or her direct reports create their own V2MOMs, and so on, until every employee has a V2MOM to guide him or her for the coming year. This is how we align individual and corporate goals and demonstrate how everyone fits into the organization. (It's also the basis for performance reviews.) It's empowering for employees to see how their work is important to the success of the company. This process is so critical to us that we have created an application on our Force.com platform called "Peopleforce," which enables us to track all of the V2MOMs. This is more than an application, though; it's become our "corporate operating system," and each update allows us to run more efficiently.

Play #102: Build a Recruiting Culture

Our very first V2MOM, written in 1999, revealed to us that our biggest obstacle was a talent deficit. We needed more developers and new product managers to help us build our service. However, the first hire I made based on that intelligence was not another developer. It was an HR manager. Although most start-ups don't hire a dedicated HR person right away, doing so made sense to me because acquiring the right talent is the most important key to growth.

The right people and the right number of people set the pace for the entire company. After all, the better the developers you have, the better the product you build. The more developers you have, the more products you can build. Essentially, recruiting is the engine that drives distribution. Therefore, hiring was—and still is—the most important thing we do.

Nancy Connery, our first HR director, set the tone for a recruiting culture that radiated throughout the entire organization. In a way, we also had the close quarters of the apartment-office to thank. Our crowded space forced different "departments" (one-person departments at the time) to mix, and everyone got swept up in the excitement and responsibility of hiring. As Nancy was going through resumes, for example, she'd come across candidates that people in other divisions already knew, and she'd solicit off-the-cuff references. That type of interdepartmental communication and collaboration was invaluable. We've continued to tap into—and trust—our network as we've grown. Social networking tools, such as LinkedIn and Facebook, make it easier than ever to establish connections, source references, and leverage everyone as members of our recruiting team.

Although we had ambitious plans when it came to hiring, we were often stymied by our competition in our start-up days. We were competing with scores of fast-hiring dot-coms for the most talented employees. These companies were spending ridiculous sums of money to recruit the best and brightest people, and several were paying signing bonuses. We couldn't afford that, so we tried all sorts of odd strategies (like radio ads) to find candidates, and we considered the diverse candidates we reeled in. One time, Rob Acker, who was on a frenzied hunt for salespeople, returned from a recruiting fair telling me about some of the candidates he'd met. Highlights included a fishing boat captain and a truck driver.

The fact was that because there was a talent shortage and we couldn't afford to pay for experience, we had to be open to hiring people without it. This led us to people who were early in their careers, but bright and very hungry. We focused on searching for raw talent that we could shape. We developed a "checks and balances" system whereby everybody had to interview and review these hires, so we felt confident that we were getting the real deal.

Hiring Checks and Balances

The first trait we looked for in new hires was attitude; the second was aptitude. We vetted candidates through multiple audit points:

- **Aggressive interviews**. We use a 360-degree interview process whereby peers and other managers interview the candidate. During our first two years in business, I was adamant that I had to meet all hires and interview all candidates as well. Everyone had to agree that the candidate was a good fit with the company DNA.

- **Presentations**. Asking candidates to present allows us to see how they perform on the fly, and especially how deftly they can handle curve balls. It works on a more subtle level, too. Preparation demonstrates how badly candidates want to be with us. We note whether or not they have been to our Web site. Are they familiar with our products? Do they know our customers?

In many ways, it was easier to mold raw talent than it would have been to retrain people with extensive industry experience. Many of the people in our industry had been brainwashed by the client-server model, and that attitude would have clashed with our culture. Ultimately we found that as long as the people we hired were motivated, they were able to rise to any challenge and could easily adapt to our new vision and aggressive goals. It turned out that many of the individuals in this fresh talent pool were better than the most seasoned people we hired, and they became some of our most successful. For example, a former assistant at a law firm whom we hired for an entry-level sales position went on to become a sales manager and one of the company's top performers.

Play #103: Recruiting Is Sales

We take hiring as seriously as we do revenue. Some people say I am obsessed with hiring, and they're right. The demand for top talent in today's market, especially in IT, is ferocious. It is not uncommon for candidates to entertain multiple offers from high-profile and well-branded organizations. We also have to compete with start-ups that are offering equity and the energizing opportunity of building something from the ground up. (If you are a small business, this is the right card to play to win the most motivated and dedicated employees.) For all businesses, no matter what size, it is necessary to come up with a compelling story in order to compete.

We apply our sales playbook to recruiting. One example is the "attraction strategy." We don't close most of our deals on price, and similarly we don't win most of our employees on compensation. We use something that has more staying power, and something that can't be copied or matched by a competitor.

In sales, for example, we sell the vision we have for the future and the opportunity to participate in building it with us. We have other pitches as well, and we take the time to research the prospect and determine which pitch will be most effective. We employ this multipitch menu in a similar way in recruiting. If we are looking for someone in development, for example, we pitch innovation and our agile development methodology. Candidates are excited to contribute to something that customers are passionate about. They are also attracted to the fact that the code they write at salesforce.com will be live in three to six months, whereas most of the code they write at Microsoft will never see the light of day.

When it comes to winning the best salespeople, we pitch opportunity. Corporate sales is the heart of our business, and we promote our program's built-in career ladder to attract candidates. If someone has a vision to be a top salesperson, she appreciates that we have a defined way to help her get there. (We find that this is of particular value in Japan, where being a top salesperson is an extremely honored position, yet local companies don't offer a defined career ladder to help people get there.)

It's not just the pitch that we borrow from sales; we also utilize the seed-and-grow philosophy. Instead of having an HR department that acquired talent, we wanted to build a machine that generated a huge pipeline of talent. To do so, we started one-on-one relationships with prospects. We kept in frequent communication with these people. In many cases, the person we were communicating with or inviting to have lunch wasn't even looking for a job (and may not even have known he was on an interview). Frequently, there wasn't even an appropriate position at our company. We knew there would be at some point, though, and we wanted to make certain that we had identified the right candidate. Later, once that person was in the door, we leveraged his relationships to lure his best colleagues over to our company.

Just as our board members are a tremendous help in connecting us to the right executives when we go on sales calls, they play an equally important role in the candidate-generation cycle. Early on, board member and investor Igor Sill recommended a great developer, Paul Nakada, who joined us as the fourth engineer during our start-up days and made many significant contributions to building the product. Other board members identified additional talent that we could not have accessed on our own. Many companies do not continue to rely on their boards as a resource for collaboration as they grow, but we've found our board to be especially valuable for identifying talent in new regions or new departments. We are still in start-up mode in many of these areas, and we can't afford to put as much cash on the line as a more established competitor. Our board relationships have given us a proven way to appeal to the hearts and minds of the best talent.

Build a Recruiting Machine

Much like our sales team, the recruiting team uses every effort possible to generate leads.

- **Don't wait for resumes to come to you**. Get the search party going. Erin Flynn, the head of worldwide recruiting, along with her staff, is always searching to identify the top 5 to 10 percent of talent at competing organizations. (Erin is on a constant talent quest, networking with everyone she hires, our board members, and people she meets at parties.)

- **Consider recruiting to be part of your job**. I am personally on the hunt for talent at all times, and still hold one meeting every day that I would consider a job interview — whether the candidate knows it or not. Whenever I meet someone interesting, I can't help but wonder if he or she would be an appropriate fit for our company. I stay connected to these people and find that many of them turn out to be possible candidate leads. On average, I forward our HR department about five e-mails a day and ask them to follow up with these potential candidates. Most of these compelling individuals would not have contacted our HR department or blindly submitted a resume, yet this is how we have won some of the most talented people on our team.

- **Include employees in the talent quest**. Employees are among the very best sources of top best talent. Talented people always know other talented people. We ask employees to assist us with connections, and we encourage everyone to refer a friend, former coworker, industry peer, or family member with whom they would want to work. As an incentive for their efforts, we offer a bonus ($2,000 to $10,000, depending on the position) if their referral is hired. It works: in 2008 alone, we hired 251 referred candidates and paid out more than half a million dollars in referral bonuses.

- **Add people to your leadership level first**. This is the right strategy in the beginning of a company's life cycle, and should remain the strategy as an organization grows. If we move into a new market or a new product, I want the most knowledgeable person — the guru — on our side. Once the guru articulates the strategy, he or she makes the necessary hires and invests the resources necessary to execute it.

Play #104: Keep Your Standards High as You Grow

In our early days, we had to sell hard to win candidates, but now we've created a place that people flock to—and more than half of the people who come to us aren't the right fit. Just as it is imperative to set the talent bar high from the beginning, it's essential to keep it just as high. As a company grows, the biggest challenge is the constant pressure to lower your hiring standards.

Hiring the best requires diligence. When we hire talent directly out of college, we look for individuals who come from the top universities and make up the top 5 percent of their class. If we are hiring someone with more experience, those rules change. We look for massive accomplishment and energy. We like employees to have an entrepreneurial drive; we like people who are scrappy; we value folks who have something to prove.

Not long ago, a guest at a salesforce.com off-site management meeting asked how many of the executives in attendance were first-generation college graduates. One-third of the people in the room raised their hands. That's a fairly large number, yet it did not surprise me. We have a highly motivated and hungry group, in part because they have never been handed anything. Those are the kind of people who fit—and propel—a high-growth organization.

How to Hire Innovators: Hire People Who Are Better Than You

Conventional wisdom says you should hire people who are *not* like you. That's wrong. Hire people who are like you, only better. Growing up, my parents always told me that to get better at tennis, I had to play with "A" players. By playing with the best, they said, my own game will improve.

We have always had a very rigorous selection process, and we have continued it as we've grown because each hire is so critical to our success. We vet people through an extensive interview process that typically includes four to five interviews, but it can swell to ten to fifteen different meetings, even for relatively low positions. (This is helpful for the candidate too. If she is intimidated, she self-selects out, which saves us time.)

Relationships, Relationships, Relationships

In the early days, I interviewed everyone who came to work at salesforce.com. That's no longer possible. I still like to have a hand in every new hire, though. It's important for me to be able to reference everyone who joins us in a leadership position, meaning that I know and trust someone he or she knows. Someone from my executive team still interviews every candidate we hire — even for the most junior positions. After all, we are looking for those junior people to grow into more senior posts, and it's critical to make sure that they align with the vision of the organization.

The (Unlikely) Number-One Characteristic You Want in a Hire

What we value most is a desire to change the world via technology and an interest in giving back to the community. We find that this desire drives the type of candidate who shares our vision. Look for candidates who appreciate your vision and share your values. These are the people who will fit best and make the most significant contributions.

High-level positions often require dozens of interviews, often with some unlikely stakeholders. When Jim Steele was interviewing for the role of president of worldwide operations, he met with thirty-six individuals, including investors, a corporate psychiatrist, my girlfriend, and my dog. This in no way slowed down the process. Jim met with each of these people over two or three weeks, and at the end of the process we were 100 percent sure he would be a good fit—and we were right.

It's very important for hiring to be consensus driven. To that end, we use the "all yes" rule. If a candidate meets ten people and nine say yes and one says no, that candidate will not work at our company. This might sound unusual, but new employees need to have the support of all the stakeholders; otherwise they will not be successful.

Play #105: How to Retain Top Talent

Getting the right people on board is an utterly useless accomplishment if you can't keep them for the long term. All new employees require a significant investment, and companies can't afford to be slowed down by people who don't work out or stay.

We've devised an extensive onboarding process to help employees achieve success. When we started, new hires had to set up their own computers (and their own desks), which was fine because we needed self-starters, but as we've evolved, so too has our orientation program. In the past number of years, we have included all new hires in a two-day orientation at our headquarters as a way to get them off to the right start. Their laptop is set up by the time they arrive, and paperwork—the bane of most orientations—is taken care of beforehand. The first day begins with a member of the executive team giving an overview of the company. The new hires meet other company leaders, learn about products and governance, and learn about V2MOM. After the final session ends, we invite everyone to dinner at a top restaurant. This makes sense because relationships are fundamental to the success of any business. Take the time to get to know one another as individuals.

Getting off to the Right Start

Encourage employees to stop by the desk of new hires to greet them and express that they are happy to see them at the company. It's a small thing that immediately makes people feel welcome and helps boost teamwork and camaraderie.

Make sure every new employee has lunch plans on his or her first day. If you or the employee's manager can't go, have another member of your team do so. It is important to set the right motivating tone from day one.

A fundamental part of our orientation—and something that should be immediately introduced to employees at any size company—is a crash course on the product and an immersion in the company culture. We offer intensive product training so that all new hires receive insight into how a typical user works with our application. In addition, we have a half-day "foundation event" in which new hires participate in a community service project, such as cleaning up a park, doing maintenance work at a homeless shelter, or serving food in a soup kitchen. This demonstrates the importance we place on giving back to our communities. It creates an opportunity for employees to think differently, employ teamwork, and work with people across departments—all concepts that are central to the way we operate.

There's also a required session on culture led by our chief creative officer, Bruce Campbell, who imparts his philosophy that "a culture is a shared vision and shared values." He teaches attendees about our culture, which is defined by a focus on the customer, standing for something, delivering on promises, and being responsive, reliable, confident, passionate, approachable, trustworthy, and fun. Brands are built and sustained on consistency. Whether employees realize it or not, everyone in a company interfaces with customers in one way or another, and their attitude will affect the brand. A wrong message or attitude from one person has the potential to dilute our brand, so we try to make sure everyone is in alignment from the beginning.

Play #106: The Importance of Mahalo

It's necessary for every company to integrate *mahalo*—the Hawaiian spirit of gratitude and praise—into its corporate culture. It's simple enough to reward employees for extra performance with extraordinary compensation and a competitive rewards portfolio, but it's really the everyday environment that contributes to people's happiness, success, and longevity at a company. When I started salesforce.com, I very clearly remembered the innovative culture of Apple and recognized that it was the small things (like the fruit smoothies) that made me more excited to go to work every day. I borrowed pieces of that when we launched salesforce.com, including a kitchen full of healthy snacks, and massages for members of the tech team as a special thank-you following each release. We also added perks that reflected our culture: a company-paid gym membership, free yoga classes with a renowned instructor, and discounted tickets on Hawaiian Airlines.

Further, we've made celebrating our collective success an important part of our culture. It motivates people, and it's fun. We offer opportunities for employees to nominate their peers for various recognition categories, and we reward the winners with $500 bonuses. Perhaps our most unusual—and visible—award recognizes distinguished employees with a life-size poster of them, which we display throughout our office. It's easy and inexpensive enough for any company to do this, and the process alone is enjoyable enough for everyone to make it worthwhile.

Conventional wisdom says that most salespeople are "coin operated," so most companies use monetary incentives to motivate top salespeople. This is essential but insufficient, as material things are not really what brings anyone true happiness. When asked about their best year, salespeople rarely point to the year in which their W-2 was the highest; they point to a year in which they were challenged and recognized, and had fun. That's why we reward any salesperson who makes 100 percent of his or her quota (and a partner or friend) with a fantastic experience—a three-day trip to Maui. Typically, 60 to 65 percent of our account executives qualify for this trip. Most companies reward only the top 10 to 20 percent of their sales reps, but that strategy doesn't yield a very high return. Morale for the top people is sky high, but it is brutally low for the 80 to 90 percent of people who are not recognized. By setting the bar within reach, we've found that morale soars all year—and people still strive to exceed expectations.

To distinguish ourselves from other employers and to further encourage people to perform, we strive to offer experiences that are memorable. That's why we came up with Breakfast at Tiffany's. Every year in Hawaii, we take the very top sales producers and their guests by limo to the Four Seasons Resort Lana'i, where each gets a personal shopper and a sponsored shopping trip to Tiffany & Co., held before the store is open to the public. An Audrey Hepburn look-alike welcomes the top performers and serves champagne.

It's important to reward people because it's the right thing to do, but the benefits come back to the company. Involving spouses or partners produces great results! Keeping them happy keeps the employees happy. Free tickets to a ball game only go so far with an employee (or a client). If you really want to make a difference, give something meaningful to an employee's significant other or child. Things that have some emotional value attached to them are what encourage people the most.

Play #107: Foster Loyalty by Doing the Right Thing

It was very distressing when Steve Garnett, who tirelessly built our business in EMEA, came to me and explained that he had been diagnosed with rheumatoid arthritis. He was surprised when I took an interest in his health care and introduced him to doctors who I believed could make a difference. I was happy to help, and it was the right thing to do. We have also benefited, though. Helping people deal with challenging issues that lie outside the business arena significantly strengthens the business relationship. Not long after we supported Steve in contending with his health issues, a competitor of salesforce.com called him and tried to lure him away. Although a promising opportunity (the company was planning an IPO) might have piqued the interest of some, the relationship Steve and I had forged made it impossible for him to consider it. "I'm flattered," he said, "but I could never go and compete with Marc."

It's important to take the high road in the situations you couldn't have predicted—the situations that haven't been mapped out by the HR handbook. Take, for example, what happened when one of our sales account executives, Scott Ebersole, was invited on the Hawaii trip awarded to the top salespeople. Scott and his wife, Wendi, left for the trip a few days early, and shortly after they arrived in Maui, Wendi, who was pregnant with twins, was rushed to the hospital, where she underwent surgery. She spent the next two weeks in critical condition, and a week later gave birth to Bryce and Kendall, each baby weighing only two pounds.

Scott needed a way to be with his family for the many weeks they'd be in Hawaii, but he also wanted to be able to work. We set him up to work remotely, but there were additional expenses—a rental apartment, a car, and food—so we also covered them. After several months, the Ebersoles went back to Atlanta. Everyone is doing great now, and that's what's most important, but as a result of helping his family in a difficult time, we earned the 100 percent loyalty of a valued employee. "Salesforce.com has made this situation as good as it could have been," Scott said. "I've always felt that I have their support, and it's made me to want to work even harder to give back."

Play #108: Challenge Your Best People with New Opportunities

The very best and brightest people can quickly overcome challenges and be ready for the next step. It's imperative to offer them new opportunities to keep them engaged and firmly committed. As much as it's necessary to define initial job positions, it's equally imperative to allow the individual to stretch in new directions.

We learned this lesson accidentally, when we needed people and did what it took to get them in the door—and moved them around later. As we grew, it became clear that the best people don't want to be confined by static job descriptions. Take, for example, the time we were hiring our first finance manager, Joe Allanson. Nancy Connery, our VP of HR, admitted to Joe that we didn't even have a name for the position, or any paperwork on it. "That's what I'm looking for: a clean piece of paper," Joe told Nancy. He had been in the same position for four years, and felt that there was nowhere to grow.

One of the best ways to keep employees engaged is to evolve positions frequently. (This is not simply in the context of dealing with someone who is not working out. It should go without saying that you would remove those people as quickly as possible.) Take the people who are dynamite in their posts and move them somewhere else. They will appreciate the new challenges, and a stale spot in your organization will be reenergized, or a new area can get off the ground.

We select our very best people and put them in new regions, move them across departments, and transfer them in and out of headquarters. As people grow and gain more access to the executive team, they have a broader perspective and a deeper understanding of our company culture, sales strategies, and marketing tactics. They can help leverage this knowledge across the company. Rotational assignments can span a few years, a few months, or just a few weeks. Even short-term experiences help employees develop new skills and perspectives.

Hire Fast, Fire Fast

You do your best to hire the right candidate, but even with great practices in place, there are inevitably some people who do not work out. They might be talented, but they are not a good fit for your organization. If possible, consider other roles for them, but don't keep them in positions that are not working.

The way to determine if it's time to let someone go is this: Would you regret it if the person resigned? If you wouldn't regret it, you should have already let him go. You want to regret the loss of everyone who walks out the door. In brief:

- Hire A players.
- Demote B players.
- Fire C players.

Play #109: Solicit Employee Feedback—and Act On It

Right before salesforce.com's IPO, we had about five hundred employees and $100 million in sales. We were interested in taking a snapshot of our company at this pivotal point so that we could see how things changed as we grew. The only way to get a truly 360-degree benchmark of our organization was to survey employees. Although I knew this was important, it was a difficult decision to commit to this effort. It would expose us to vulnerabilities, and the results would be a reflection on management. I thought employees would be skeptical as well. Would they perceive management as wanting to use the survey results for malicious reasons (to identify dissatisfied employees or to weed out weak supervisors)? Would people really participate?

I expressed my concerns to David Youssefnia, the founder of Critical Metrics, a Web-based survey company. "You don't want a survey to have negative energy around it; you have to embrace it," David told me. "When a survey is conducted in a climate of mistrust, it is understandable that employees may think management may use the survey for nefarious purposes." David stressed the importance of being open with employees about how the results would and wouldn't be used. He argued that if we shared our findings—and action plans—the process could build trust between management and employees.

I wasn't sure. However, I *was* sure that that this represented a transition to becoming a more mature company. Of the Fortune 500 companies, 70 percent survey employees, and of the twenty-five companies named the best medium-size places to work in America, 92 percent conduct employee surveys.[1] We conducted our first survey in spring 2005, not long after the IPO. We learned that although everyone was excited about the company and focused on the customer, employees weren't sure about the longevity of their careers with us.

"I'm doing the best work of my career," employees stated in the survey. "Now I want to figure out how to be a lifer." A lifer? That wasn't something we ever thought about at salesforce.com. Lifers were employees they had at Hewlett-Packard or IBM. Yet our employees were demanding to know what was in store for them in the long term.

Salesforce.com had placed little importance on formal career development. We realized now that we had to focus on it. Our employees needed more clearly defined opportunities to grow. The company could also benefit by developing a robust pipeline of internal candidates.

The revelations from the survey responses led us to add another level of management to give people more opportunities for development and growth. It also prompted us to hone our continuing education program. One example was a "black belt" series of quarter-long classes taught by executives and veteran employees who were able to take their salesfore.com expertise and pass it on. For instance, our VP of corporate

Benchmark for Employee Success

We use this checklist to measure our success as leaders and managers. We strive to create opportunities so that all our employees are able to check off the following:

- ❏ I am doing the best work of my professional career.
- ❏ I have the opportunity to do what I do best every day at work.
- ❏ In the past six months, I have talked with someone about my progress.
- ❏ There is someone at work who encourages my development.
- ❏ I have opportunities to learn and grow at work.
- ❏ My opinions are sought after and seem to count.
- ❏ My supervisor, or someone at work, seems to care about me as a person.
- ❏ I have a support network at work.
- ❏ My coworkers are committed to doing quality work.
- ❏ I am recognized and rewarded for my contributions.

strategy, Bruce Francis, taught a class called Shock and Awe: Positioning and PR. Employees were eager to learn from executives and internal leaders. In fact, the black belt program in marketing has been oversubscribed, yielding a wait list each quarter.

By the time we conducted the next survey, we received much higher marks for training and development. The survey successfully identified pain points, and we came up with solutions. In that sense, the use of surveys surpassed my expectations, not only by providing a baseline indicator but also by serving as a strategic planning tool.

Play #110: Leverage Everything

The power of leverage is a constant theme at salesforce.com. We leverage our customers' energy to evangelize and sell our product; we leverage our resources (equity, product, time) to give back to the community; we leverage our employees' networks to tap the best talent.

In a similar way, we leverage the skills of outside organizations to help service, sell, and build our product (and an economy around our product). In the beginning, we did all the support and services in-house. As our suite of services grew and our customers became larger and their needs more complex, we began to leverage outside talent to help support them as well. Consultancies like Bluewolf and Astadia cropped up, taking a bet on cloud computing services like salesforce.com and offering their skills to help companies get up and running and maximize these services. This was a very exciting development. Our reach, resources, and capabilities stretched with the commitment of these partners. We had to nourish and develop this network. The way to do this was by empowering individuals and building a community around them.

To that end, we launched a training and certification program to help build a self-sustainable group of experts around our product. (We made training flexible by offering it both online and offline in classrooms.) This effort gave us a way to ensure that their skills were at the highest level, and it also provided a way to validate their work. The practice of offering certifications is not new. Microsoft does this, and in fact, while I was at Oracle, we launched a database administration certification system. Industry-recognized certifications allow partners and independent software vendors and administrators to advance their skill sets, as well as improve job security, career advancement, and compensation opportunities. Employers use certification as a litmus test, as do customers who find value in knowing that they are engaging consultants of a certain standard.

As much as certification creates value for the individual, it results in real value for your company. If people are learning and earning on a certain system, they want to take it with them wherever they go. This encourages them to further evangelize your service, and allows you to grow your business.

Using education as a way to extend our service and expand our capabilities is our strategy for future growth. It comes down to simple mathematics: we can hire one hundred developers to develop new functionality, or we can hire ten trainers who have the capacity to train thousands of developers. Leveraging the power of trainers has allowed us to have thousands of developers creating new functionality, sharing it in our online marketplace, and enabling us to offer a more comprehensive service to our customers.

Think about the partners that might recommend your service and the vendors that might build complementary products; then, do everything you can to strengthen the entire ecosystem that surrounds your company. In doing so, you can turn a handful of disjointed partners into a thriving community of supporters, innovators, and evangelists that will further your success.

The Final Play

Play #111: Make Everyone Successful

A little over a decade ago, Clayton Christensen wrote a book called *The Innovator's Dilemma*. It illustrated how a start-up company—by employing innovation that disrupts existing business models—will always beat the established big companies. He cited examples like Intel's success with the microprocessor and the steel mill Nucor's hit with its revolutionary way to reuse scrap. The book was loathed by the old-line folks and lauded by the new guys like me. It validated us for what we knew was right: the future wasn't about simply improving on what was already done; it was about being bold enough to make big, sweeping, dramatic changes.

With those ideas in mind, I started salesforce.com with a mission to do enterprise software differently. At the time, companies were paying hundreds of thousands to buy and millions to install applications that were costly and frustrating to maintain. We wanted to take advantage of a new platform—the Internet—and deliver business applications cheaply through a Web site that was as easy to use as Amazon.com. We had to think out of the box. Literally, no more packaged software. And figuratively, as no one was then selling subscriptions for business applications and delivering them over the Web.

The success of our End of Software mission allowed us to promote other agendas—specifically, a goal to change corporate philanthropy from simply writing a check to leveraging all a corporation's resources. Our 1-1-1 model (1 percent of our equity, 1 percent of our time, and 1 percent of our profits through product donation) has allowed us to donate $14 million in grants, deliver our service to over six thousand nonprofits at no charge, and give more than 150,000 hours of community service.

This mandate also changed our company. It established us as a meaningful place to work and made us more committed to the success of our employees and our customers. The final play from our salesforce.com playbook—#111—acknowledges that through making all our stakeholders successful, we ignited our own success.

In all industries, especially the technology industry, people overestimate what you can do in one year, and they underestimate what you can do in ten. As I write this on salesforce.com's tenth anniversary, I understand just how true that is. In 1999, I recruited three developers, rented an empty apartment, brought in a few computers, and turned the bedroom closet into a data center. We soon had a prototype of the service running, and over the next few months a steady stream of new employees, potential users, investors, and reporters came by to see what was happening and share their insights to help us build something better.

That first year was exhilarating—and exhausting. No one prepared us for the unexpected obstacles. There were times we thought we wouldn't make it. Now, ten years later, our small company is a big one. The few initial employees who gave salesforce.com everything have grown into a few thousand employees. Revenue has escalated to more than $1 billion a year.

We look very different today, but so does the rest of the world. Whereas we once had to educate the market about our "no software" model, an industry known as cloud computing has grown up around us and changed everything. Gartner estimates the current market for cloud services is $46.4 billion, and by 2013, the market will reach $150.1 billion.[1] The SaaS market we evangelized is now growing twice as fast as the enterprise software market. It has spawned countless new companies. We might be the first SaaS company to reach $1 billion in revenue, but we won't be alone for long. "Today IDC estimates that there are more than 1,000 worldwide SaaS providers and more than $33 billion has been invested in SaaS providers globally," says Robert Mahowald, director of SaaS and On Demand Research at IDC.

We've always believed that everything was going into the cloud because it was a model that allowed everyone to succeed. Now, in precarious times, we know that the advantages of cloud computing (less risk, no capital expenditure, predictable operating expenses, and fast results) will further spur adoption. (Case in point: in the last quarter of 2008 and the first quarter of 2009, when most technology companies were battling revenue declines, we increased revenue by 34 percent and 23 percent, respectively, over the same periods in the prior years.)

Now we are most excited by how the industry's growth will unleash further innovation. The cost of technology is continually lowering while becoming easier to use. Tremendous advances with handheld devices and wireless Internet access will continue to increase cloud computing and social networking. This only makes the future more exciting for everyone, as it's always been through advances in technology that we have solved complex problems and improved our lives.

Many entrepreneurs have serious concerns in these unprecedented times. I understand, as I had similar worries about my business during the last period of economic uncertainty. Having survived the dot-com disaster to build the fastest-growing technology stock on the NYSE, I know that marketplaces are more receptive to change in challenging times. Salesforce.com is hardly alone in what it has accomplished out of adversity. GE, Cisco, Southwest Airlines, and other disruptive companies were started in depressions or recessions. As the Eskimo proverb goes, "the storm is the time to fish."

Now is not the time to cut back on a commitment to innovation, creativity, and altruism. That's what's needed to build a brighter future. We have a responsibility to keep going. Innovation, which led to new companies that employed people, created wealth, and sparked economic growth, is the way we overcame the past economic crises—and it is what will save us again.

We all have an opportunity to play a role in improving the state of the world. I urge you to build game-changing businesses—wildly innovative, profitable, scalable, and sustainable businesses—that offer imaginative solutions to the problems we face.

It is my hope that you will use your business acumen, your creativity, your passion, and the 111 plays in this book to make a positive difference. I'm not asking you not to make money. On the contrary, go out and make money—and lots of it. But know that simply making money will not be enough to sustain you. No one who is successful is driven solely by monetary rewards. The most successful businesspeople are driven by profits—and purpose.

Back in high school, when I started my first business, I worked under a poster of Albert Einstein. Because I found inspiration from it, I hung another picture of Einstein in the apartment when we launched salesforce.com. We weren't always aware of it, but we were guided by his three rules of work: 1) Out of clutter find simplicity; 2) From discord find harmony; 3) In the middle of difficulty lies opportunity.

We are now in a time of extraordinary opportunity. People always ask me, What's in store for the future? Where is technology going? Where is philanthropy going? Predicting the future is simple. The future is whatever we imagine. We all must think three years out, five years out, ten years out. What's ahead of us is whatever we create.

What do you see in the future? I see less disease. I see less poverty. I see alternative sources of energy, innovative clean technologies, and a planet on which the next generation can still breathe. I see hope because I know there's a corps of talented people who can help us make the types of bold changes that are necessary.

Seize the opportunity in front of you. Imagine. Invent. Disrupt. Do good. I know that you must be passionate, unreasonable, and a little bit crazy to follow your own ideas and do things differently. But it's worth it. Life grows relative to one's investment in it. I promise you that by considering everyone's success, you will see the return.

I wish you great success. I look forward to hearing about the future you predict—and living in the one you create.

Aloha, Marc

Notes

Part 1

1. Nicholas Carr, *The Big Switch: Rewiring the World, from Edison to Google,* New York: Norton, 2008, http://www.nicholasgcarr.com/bigswitch/.

2. The Yankee Group. "Mid-Market CRM Total Cost of Ownership: Noodling the Numbers," Customer Relationship Strategies, Vol. 3, No. 6, June 2001.

3. Gartner, Inc., "SaaS at the Forefront of the Consumerization of IT," May 8, 2007, http://www.gartner.com/Display Document?id=505054&ref=g_sitelink.

Part 2

1. Don Clark, "Canceled Programs: Software Is Becoming an Online Service, Shaking Up an Industry—Users Tapping Applications on the Web Force Firms to Reconfigure

Strategy—A Threat to Wintel's Power?" *Wall Street Journal*, July 21, 1999, A1.

2. Damien Cave, "Dot-Com Party Madness," Salon.com, April 25, 2000, http://archive.salon.com/tech/feature/2000/04/25/party/index.html.

3. Matt Hines, "Salesforce.com's Brash New Ads Reflect the Style of Its Leader," SearchCRM.com, March 13, 2002, http://searchcrm.techtarget.com/news/article/0,289142,sid11_gci809857,00.html.

Part 3

1. David Berlind, "Full Text of Marc Benioff's Internal Memo to Salesforce Staff on Oracle/Siebel Deal," *Between the Lines*, September 12, 2005, blogs.ZDNet.com.

Part 5

1. Rochelle Garner, "Microsoft Undermined by Salesforce.com in Web Sales," Bloomberg.com, Jan. 25, 2008, http://www.bloomberg.com/apps/news?pid=20601087&sid=afUTE1bpZWp4&refer=home.

2. Jeff Howe, *Crowdsourcing: Why the Power of the Crowd Is Driving the Future of Business*, New York: Crown Business, 2008, p. 158.

3. Jeff Jarvis, "Hey Starbucks, How About Coffee Cubes?" *BusinessWeek*, April 15, 2008, http://www.businessweek.com/magazine/content/08_17/b4081000030457.htm.

4. Jeff Jarvis, "Dell Learns to Listen," *BusinessWeek*, October 17, 2007, http://www.businessweek.com/bwdaily/dnflash/content/oct2007/db20071017_277576.htm.

5. Spencer Reiss, "Planet Amazon," *Wired*, May 16, 2008, http://www.wired.com/techbiz/it/magazine/16-05/mf_amazon?currentPage=all.

Part 6

1. Carlye Adler, "The Fresh Prince of Software," *FSB: Fortune Small Business*, March 1, 2003, http://money.cnn.com/magazines/fsb/fsb_archive/2003/03/01/338759/index.htm.

Part 8

1. U.S. Bank Study, 2004. Brad Sugars, "The 6 Biggest Mistakes in Raising Startup Capital," *Entrepreneur*, September. 20, 2007, http://www.entrepreneur.com/startingabusiness/startupbasics/startupbasicscolumnistbradsugars/article184350.html.

2. Michael S. Malone and Shelley Pannill, "The Best VCs," *Forbes ASAP*, May 29, 2000, http://www.forbes.com/asap/2000/0529/098.html.

3. Wasabi Ventures, "Raising Venture Capital: A Primer for 1st Time Entrepreneurs," http://blog.wasabiventures.com/raising-venture-capital-a-primer-for-1st-time-entrepreneurs/.

4. William Bygrave and Andrew Zacharakis, *Entrepreneurship*, Hoboken: John Wiley & Sons, 2007, pp. 64, 346.

5. Jeffrey Sohl, "The Angel Investor Market in 2008: A Down Year In Investment Dollars But Not In Deals," Center for Venture Research, March 26, 2008, http://www.innovationamerica.us/index.php/publications-and-presentations/published-reports/75-the-angel-investor-market-in-2008-a-down-year-in-investment-dollars-but-not-in-deals.

Part 9

1. "50 Best Small & Medium Companies to Work for in America," *HR Magazine*, July 2006, http://findarticles .com/p/articles/mi_m3495/is_7_53/ai_n27932757/.

The Final Play

1. Gartner, Inc., "Forecast: Sizing the Cloud; Understanding the Opportunities in Cloud Services," March 18, 2009, http://www.gartner.com/DisplayDocument?id=914826.

Acknowledgments

It's no secret that I like to think big. Still, the success of salesforce.com has even surpassed my wildest expectations. This has been the most exciting decade of my life, in every way, and there have been many people who have given everything to join me on this adventure. I have many people to thank.

I am immensely grateful to three talented developers—Parker Harris, Frank Dominguez, and Dave Moellenhoff—who in 1999 took a risk on a "crackpot idea," and then built something spectacular.

To all the people from the earliest days who left stability and took a chance with me, especially John Appleby, Jim Burleigh, Steve Cakebread, Nancy Connery, Shelly Davenport, John Dillon, Jim Emerich, Andy Hyde, Fergus Gloster, Diane Mark, Caryn Marooney, Paul Nakada, Tien Tzou, and Mitch Wallace.

Salesforce.com is a different company today than it was ten years ago, and I'm appreciative of the people who have helped us become better and who continue to push us to evolve: Tom Addis, Joe Allanson, Krista Anderson, Lindsey Armstrong, Tom Berson, Bruce Campbell, Jim Cavalieri, Linda Crawford, Dan Dal Degan, Alexandre Dayon, David Dempsey, Steve Fisher, Erin Flynn, Steve Garnett, Sue Goble, Parker Harris, George Hu, Kenneth Juster, Hilarie Koplow-McAdams, Steve Lucas, Brian Millham, Allen Miner, Martin Moran, Brett Queener, David Rudnitsky, Carl Schachter, David Schellhase, Graham Smith, Clarence So, Jim Steele, Susan St. Ledger, Polly Sumner, John Taschek, Eiji Uda, Frank van Veenendaal, Craig Weissman, and Kirsten Wolberg.

Additionally, salesforce.com is fortunate to have an amazing board of directors: Craig Conway, Alan Hassenfeld, Craig Ramsey, Sanford Robertson, Stratton Sclavos, Larry Tomlinson, Maynard Webb, and Shirley Young.

I set out to write this book to help and inspire entrepreneurs. My story and this book would never have been realized without the many individuals who instructed and inspired me. I'm lucky to have so many true mentors who offered wisdom and support and then generously encouraged me to pursue my vision in my own way: Larry Ellison, Charlie Moore, Colin Powell, Chikara Sano, Tony Robbins, and Ammachi.

Thank you Michael Dell, a legendary entrepreneur, technologist, and philanthropist, who has contributed an inspiring foreword and who continually helps us see a better future. Thank you as well to Andy Lark, who was available and insightful no matter where he was in the world, and no matter what else he had happening.

A most special thank you to Tim Lynn, my college roommate and now our chief of staff, and to the talented and patient Laura Pavlovich, who handles everything and does it all flawlessly.

Hundreds of people have had a hand in recalling their memories, editing pages, and the making of this book. I am grateful to each and every one. Many went above and beyond the call of duty and deserve special recognition: Rob Acker, Dana Booth, Bruce Cleveland, Bruce Francis, Jane Hynes, Suzanne DiBianca, John Durocher, Doug Farber, Chris Fry, Jamie Grenney, Anne Kveta Haack, Aaron Katz, Isabel Kelly, Charles Nikiel, Elizabeth Pinkham, Joseph Schmidt, Rich Sheridan, Julie Trell, and Mayuwa Yamakawa.

I am most grateful to my extraordinary friends who supported salesforce.com and me from the very beginning and who continue to amaze me with their wise counsel and generous spirit: Adam Bosworth, Gigi Brisson, Katrina and Terry Garnett, Evan Goldberg, Mark Goldstein, Arjun Gupta, Steve McAdams, Halsey Minor, Eric Schmidt, Klaus Schwab, Igor Sill, Robert Thurman, David Vaskevitch, Bobby Yazdani, and Magdalena Yesil. I'm grateful to Lance Secretan and Neil Young, newer friends who have been tremendously supportive of salesforce.com, this book, and all endeavors.

The following special people had influences far greater than they likely ever knew. Each one is deeply missed: Chris Bonacore, Jim Gray, Osamu Igarashi, Eirik Prosser, and Karen Southwick.

Thank you Rick Cohen and Tanya Viner at Buchalter Nemer and Aaron Alter and Boris Feldman at Wilson Sonsini Goodrich & Rosati, true professionals who provide solid counsel that helps me sleep better and who have proven to moonlight as fine editors as well.

ACKNOWLEDGMENTS

I've been lucky enough to meet some of the best people in the world of publishing. By dedicating two years of her life and spirit, Carlye Adler made this book a reality. I'm thankful for super agent Jim Levine and his team at Levine Greenberg. A heartfelt and indebted thank-you to the very gifted Karen Murphy, development editor extraordinaire Erin Moore, production guru Mark Karmendy, copy editor Michele Jones, and the entire team at Jossey-Bass who brought this book to life.

Our success would not have been possible without our hundreds of business partners, thousands of employees, and more than a million customers. Thank you for becoming a part of our family and for your support. A special thank you to Andy Brown, Gary Butler, Cris Conde, John Chambers, Guy Chiarello, Greg Case, Gene Hall, Rick Justice, Hermann Lamberti, Harry McMahon, Haruo Murase, Bob Ridout, Keiji Torii, Steve Schuckenbrock, James Sheppard, Kazuhiko Yoshimoto, and Monte Zweben.

My family—my grandmother, my parents, my sisters—has supported me and shared invaluable lessons in life, business, and altruism that have guided me always and still do today. And Leia, who reminds me every day about what's most important.

Finally, thank you Lynne, for everything.

Mahalo Nui Loa, Marc

About the Authors

Marc Benioff is chairman and CEO of salesforce.com (NYSE: CRM), which he founded in 1999. Under Benioff's direction, salesforce.com has grown from a groundbreaking idea to the leader in enterprise cloud computing.

For its revolutionary approach, salesforce.com has received a *Wall Street Journal* Technology Innovation Award, been lauded as one of *BusinessWeek*'s Top 100 Most Innovative Companies, named No. 7 on The Wired 40, and selected in 2007 and 2008 as a Top Ten Disrupter by *Forbes*. Benioff has been widely recognized for pioneering innovation with honors such as the 2007 Ernst & Young Entrepreneur of the Year and the SDForum Visionary Award, and has been ranked on the Top 100 Most Influential People in IT survey by *eWeek* and the Top 10 Greatest IT Chief Executives by VNU. He was appointed by President George W. Bush as the co-chairman of the President's Information Technology Advisory Committee and served from 2003–2005, overseeing the publishing of critical reports on health care information technology, cybersecurity, and computational sciences.

In 2000, Benioff launched the Salesforce.com Foundation—now a multimillion-dollar global organization—establishing the "1-1-1 model," whereby the company contributes one percent of profits, one percent of equity, and one percent of employee hours back to the communities it serves. The World Economic Forum named Benioff as one of its Young Global Leaders, and in 2007 the Committee Encouraging Corporate Philanthropy presented Benioff with the coveted Excellence in Corporate Philanthropy Award. Salesforce.com has been voted one of the world's most ethical companies by *Business Ethics Magazine,* one of the best companies to work for by *Fortune,* and in 2008, Benioff was awarded CEO of the Year Award by *CRO Magazine.*

Benioff is also the author of *The Business of Changing the World* and *Compassionate Capitalism.*

Prior to launching salesforce.com, Benioff spent thirteen years at Oracle Corporation. He founded his first company, Liberty Software, when he was fifteen years old. He lives in San Francisco, California.

Carlye Adler is an award-winning journalist whose articles have appeared in *BusinessWeek, Condé Nast Portfolio, Fast Company, Fortune, Time, Wired,* and many other publications. She co-wrote, with salesforce.com chairman and CEO Marc Benioff, *The Business of Changing the World: Twenty Great Leaders on Strategic Corporate Philanthropy.* She has been twice named one of the most influential business journalists under the age of 30 by The Journalist & Financial Reporting (TJFR) Group. Her story on the hefty price of investing in a Krispy Kreme franchise was selected for inclusion in *The Best Business Stories of the Year, 2003 Edition.* She lives in New York City.

Index

INDEX

Index

Leveraging: business partnerships, 59; competition, 60–61; internal/external resources, 252–254; times of change, 82–85
Levi Strauss & Co., 140, 141
Liberty Software, 121
Licensing software, 6
Liedtke, Michael, 31
Light-and-love philosophy, 188–192
LincVolt, 229
Listening: to constituents, 148–152; to customers, 13–14, 85–86
LiveOps, 161
Local experts, 181
Local leaders: building new markets with, 187–188; injecting with corporate spirit, 170–172
LookSmart, 82

M

Mahalo, 244–246
Mahowald, Robert, 257
Mark, Diane, 70
Market leaders: engaging, 39–40
Marketing: becoming market leader, 66; branding and, 32; cultural sensitivity in, 196–198; developing strategies, 37–38; differentiating company, 28–31; engaging market leaders, 39–40; establishing product relevance, 60, 63–64; going after market leaders, 34, 36–38; including employees in, 33–34, 35; introductory parties and, 25–27; making into story, 40–41; matching to intended goals, 223; metaphors for, 44; model for, 44–45; persona for, 27–28; positioning and, 23–25; product innovations and, 60, 103–106; relationships with journalists, 41–44
Marketing. *See also* Branding
Marooney, Caryn, 24
Mata Amritananadamayi (Ammachi), 2–3, 136
McGraw-Hill, 89
Measures, 227, 228
Menefee, Douglas, 123
Mentors, 14–15, 19, 31, 137
Merck & Co., 143
Merrill Lynch, 95
Metaphors for marketing, 44
Methods, 226, 228
Metrics: basing marketing on, 44–45; criticisms of, 227, 228; market segmenting and, 80–81; measuring employee success, 251; monitoring success with, 101; revenue vs. profitability, 208–209
MGM, 203
Microloan Foundation, 157
Microsoft, 42, 43, 66, 172, 176, 253
Microsoft Hotmail, 20, 105
Millham, Brian, 83
Miner, Allen, 180–181
Minor, Halsey, 205
Mizuho Information Research, 185

Moellenhoff, Dave, 9–10, 11, 21, 106–107, 117–118, 139–140
Monster.com, 53
Moore, Charlie, 217–218
Morale, 245
Morgan Stanley, 123
Multiforce, 122
Murase, Haruo, 184–185
MyStarbucksIdea.com, 120, 129

N

Nakada, Paul, 12, 237–238
National Geographic Society, 167
NativeEnergy, 155, 162
Negotiating sales terms, 94
Nestlé, 167
Netscape, 89
NetSuite, 161
Networking, 56
New York Stock Exchange, 153, 210–211, 212–213, 217, 258
New York Times, 41, 215–217, 220
Newsom, Gavin, 152
Nikkei, 185
No Software logo, 28–29, 32
Nucor, 255

O

OASIS (Oracle Automatic Sales and Automatic Systems), 5
Obstacles: correcting, 233–236; recognizing strategic, 226–227, 228
1–1–1 Model: corporate structure for, 164–165; developing globally, 178; evolution of, 141–144; in-kind product donations, 156–158, 166; involving others in, 159–161; sharing publically, 146–147; success of, 256
Operation Smile, 141
Oprah Winfrey Show, 138
Oracle, 5, 14–16, 30–31, 63, 64, 104, 109, 137, 170–172, 179, 225–226, 253
Oracle's Promise, 137, 140, 145
OutCast Communications, 24, 33

P

PaaS (Platform-as-a-Service): AppExchange and, 125–126; developing applications with, 123–125; extending SaaS with, 122–123
Page, Larry, 160–161
PalmOne, 161
Panozza, Kevin, 190–191
Paperwork for sales, 94
Partnerships: collaborating with, 131–132; leveraging business, 59
Passion, 16
PayPal, 160, 172

275